Recreational
BICYCLE
TRAILS
of
Wisconsin

An American Bike Trails Publication

Recreational
Bicycle Trails
of Wisconsin

Published By   American Bike Trails
1157 South Milwaukee Avenue
Libertyville, IL 60048

Created by   Ray Hoven
Designed by   Boris Sorokin

Table of Contents

Table of Contents *(continued)*

How to Use This Book

This book provides a comprehensive, easy to use quick reference to the many recreational trails throughout the state of Wisconsin. It contains over 50 detailed trail maps, plus southern, central, and northern Wisconsin sectional map overviews. Following each sectional overview are the detailed trail maps located within that area. In the back of the book is an alphabetical listing of trails, plus a cross-reference listing of trails by county and town. There is also a section listing the mountain biking opportunities in Wisconsin along with pertinent information. Each trail map includes such helpful features as location and accesses, trail facilities, nearby communities, and their populations.

Terms Used

Length	Expressed in miles. Round trip mileage is normally indicated for loops.
Effort Levels	***Easy*** Physical exertion is not strenuous. Climbs and descents as well as technical obstacles are more minimal. Recommended for beginners.
	Moderate Physical exertion is not excessive. Climbs and Descents can be challenging. Expect some technical obstacles
	Difficult Physical exertion is demanding. Climbs and Descents require good riding skills. Trail surface may be sandy, loose rock, soft or wet.
Directions	Describes by way of directions and distances, how to get to the trail areas from roads and nearby communities.
Map	Illustrative representation of a geographic area, such as a state, section, forest, park or trail complex.
Forest	Typically encompasses a dense growth of trees and underbrush covering a large tract.
Park	A tract of land generally including woodlands and open areas.
DNR	Department of Natural Resources

Types of Biking

Mountain	Fat-tired bikes are recommended. Ride may be generally flat but then with a soft, rocky or wet surface.
Leisure	Off-road gentle ride. Surface is generally paved or screened.
Tour	Riding on roads with motorized traffic or on road shoulders.

Riding Tips

Pushing in gears that are too high can push knees beyond their limits. Avoid extremes by pedaling faster rather than shifting into a higher gear.

Keeping your elbows bent, changing your hand position frequently and wearing bicycle gloves all help to reduce the numbness or pain in the palm of the hand from long-distance riding.

Keep you pedal RPM's up on an uphill so you have reserve power if you lose speed.

Stay in a high-gear on a level surface, placing pressure on the pedals and resting on the handle bars and saddle.

Lower your center of gravity on a long or steep downhill run by using the quick release seat post binder and dropping the saddle height down.

Brake intermittently on a rough surface.

Wear proper equipment. Wear a helmet that is approved by the Snell Memorial Foundation or the American National Standards Institute. Look for one of their stickers inside the helmet.

Use a lower tire inflation pressure for riding on unpaved surfaces. The lower pressure will provide better tire traction and a more comfortable ride.

Apply your brakes gradually to maintain control on loose gravel or soil.

Ride only on trails designated for bicycles or in areas where you have the permission of the landowner.

Be courteous to hikers or horseback riders on the trail, they have the right-of-way.

Leave riding trails in the condition you found them. Be sensitive to the environment. Properly dispose of your trash. If you open a gate, close it behind you.

Don't carry items or attach anything to your bicycle that might hinder your vision or control.

Don't wear anything that restricts your hearing.

Don't carry extra clothing where it can hang down and jam in a wheel.

Explanation of Symbols

FACILITIES

P	Parking
👫	Restrooms
🪑	Picnic Area
🚰	Water
🍴	Refreshments
?	Information
🛏	Lodging
⛺	Camping
🏠	Shelter
+	First Aid
🔧	Bicycle Service
⛵	Boat Launch
MF	Multi-Facilities Available

First Aid   Lodging
Picnic   Refreshments
Restrooms   Telephone

TRAIL TYPES

————	Bicycle Trail
– – – –	Bikeway
┅┅┅┅	Planned Trail
▪ ▪ ▪ ▪	Hiking
= = = = =	X-C Skiing
+++++++	Railway
▬▬▬▬	Roadway

State section indication
on page in orange.
Trail location indicated by dot •

TRAIL USES

🚴	Leisure Biking
🚵	Mountain Biking
🎿	Cross-Country Skiing
🚶	Hiking
⛸	In-Line Skating
🐎	Horseback Riding
🛷	Snowmobiling

ROADS

45	Interstate Highway
45	US Highway
45	State Highway
JJ	County Highway

W —⊕— E   Directional

MILE SCALE

0   1   2   3   4   5

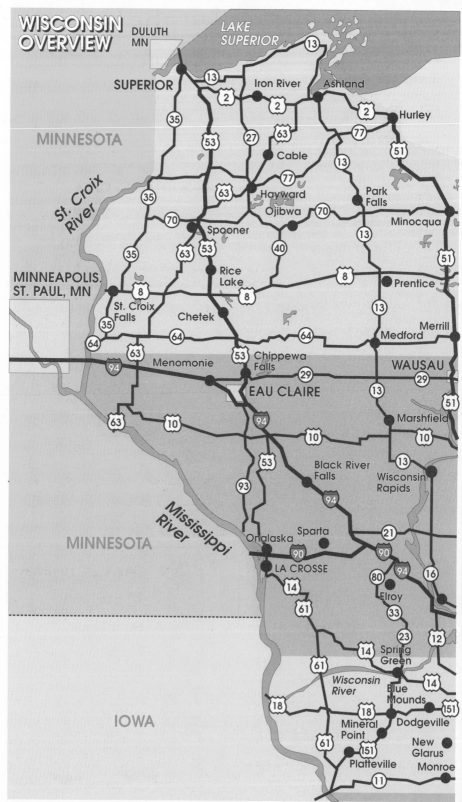

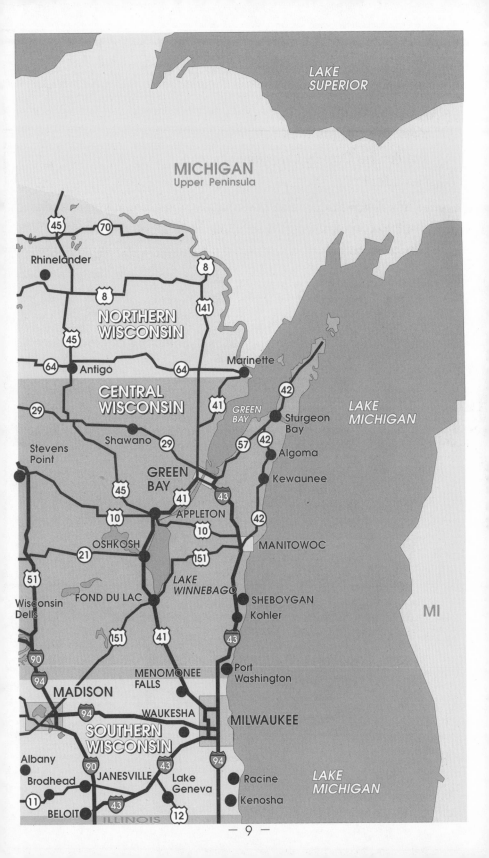

LAKE SUPERIOR

MICHIGAN
Upper Peninsula

45
70
Rhinelander
8
8
141
NORTHERN
WISCONSIN
45
64
64
Antigo
Marinette
42
CENTRAL
WISCONSIN
41
GREEN BAY
29
Sturgeon Bay
57
42
Shawano
29
Algoma
LAKE MICHIGAN
Stevens Point
GREEN BAY
Kewaunee
45
41
43
10
APPLETON
42
10
OSHKOSH
MANITOWOC
21
151
51
LAKE WINNEBAGO
Wisconsin Dells
FOND DU LAC
SHEBOYGAN
Kohler
151
41
90
43
94
MENOMONEE FALLS
Port Washington
MADISON
94
WAUKESHA
MILWAUKEE
SOUTHERN WISCONSIN
Albany
90
JANESVILLE
43
94
Brodhead
Lake Geneva
Racine
11
43
Kenosha
LAKE MICHIGAN
BELOIT
12
ILLINOIS

MI

- 9 -

Southern Wisconsin Overview

MINNESOTA

IOWA

Wisconsin Dells

90 94

Richland Center

61 14

Pine River Trail

Spring Green 23

12

12

Prairie du Chien

Wisconsin River

Fennimore

Military Ridge Trl.

Blue Mounds

18

18 151

Mineral Point

61

Dodgeville

151

Cheese Country Trail

New Glarus

Platteville

Pecatonica Trail

Calamine

Mississippi River

151

Cheese Country Trail

Monroe

11

ILLINOIS

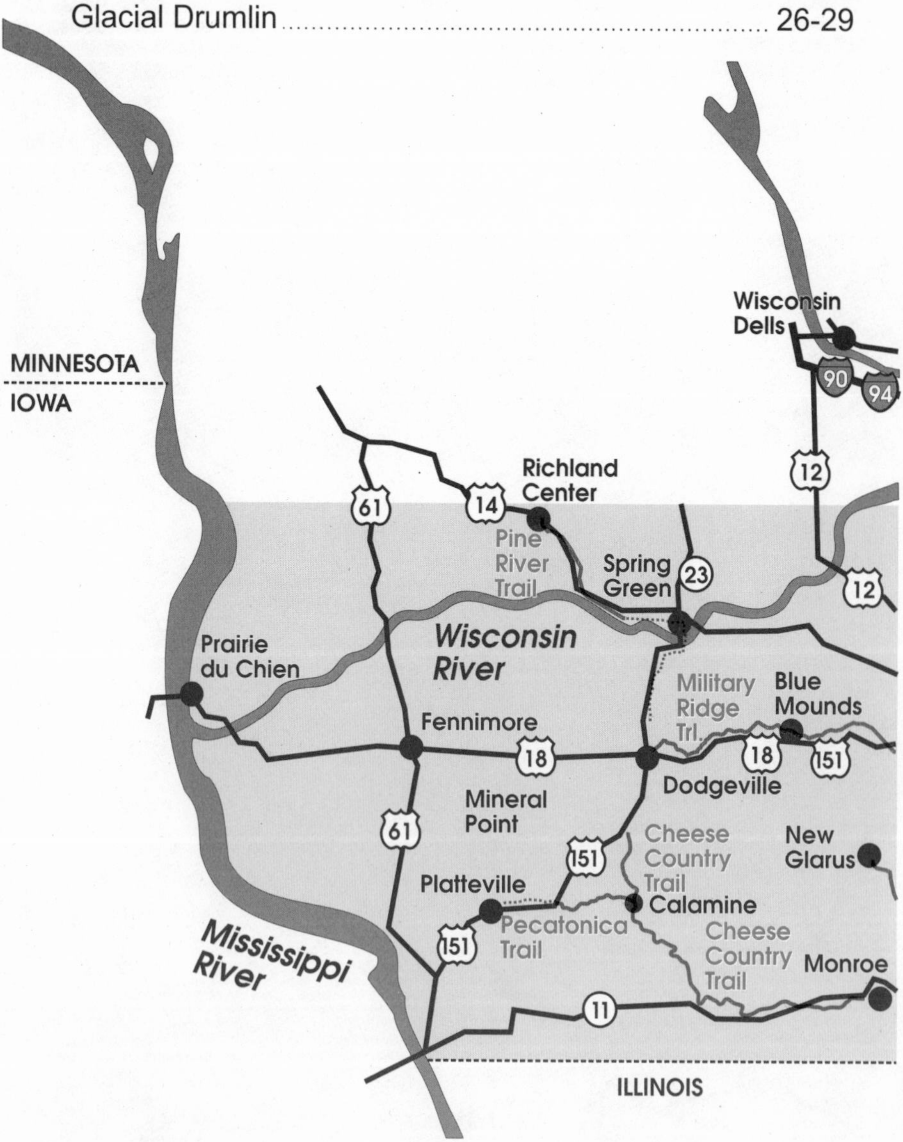

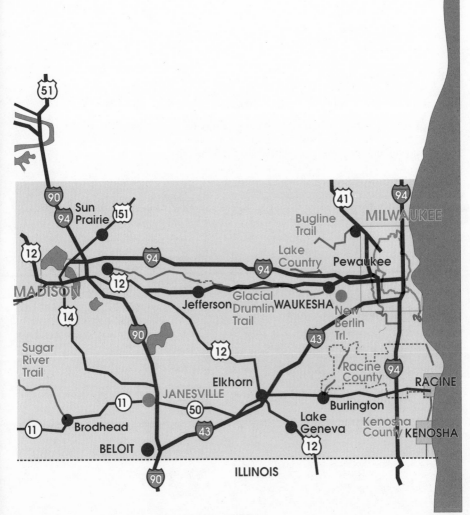

Milwaukee County Trails

Trail Length	Off-road	35.8 miles
	Parkway drives	31.0 miles
	Municipal streets	31.0 miles

Surface — Asphalt paths, streets

Uses — Bicycling, in-line skating, hiking/jogging

Location & Setting — Milwaukee County is located on the shores of Lake Michigan in southeastern Wisconsin. The city of Milwaukee is the 17th largest in the United States. The off-road paths are found in the parks and parkways that encompass the County

Information — Milwaukee County Dept. of Parks & Recreation 414/257-4501
9480 Watertown Road, Wauwatosa, WI 53226

Milwaukee County Visitors Bureau 414/273-3950

County — Milwaukee

Milwaukee derives its name from "Millocki" which means "Gathering Place by the Waters." It was here that native American Indians met for their summer encampments.

Milwaukee is made up of many ethnic neighborhoods, suburban communities, and historic districts. There are numerous festivals and ethnic celebrations from late spring through the fall.

MILWAUKEE COUNTY ZOO

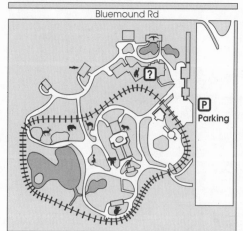
Bluemound Rd

Milwaukee County trails and bikeways are posted with directional signs.

Two types of signs mark your route:
The red, white, and blue "76" sign commemorates the national bicentennial.

EMERGENCY ASSISTANCE — **- DIAL 911**

INFORMATION
Greater Milwaukee Visitors Bureau - 800/231-0903
Local number - 414/273-3950
Milwaukee County Transit Info - 414/344-6711
Milwaukee Parks Info Hot Line - 414/257-6100

The green and white "bike route" sign is used in combination with the "76".

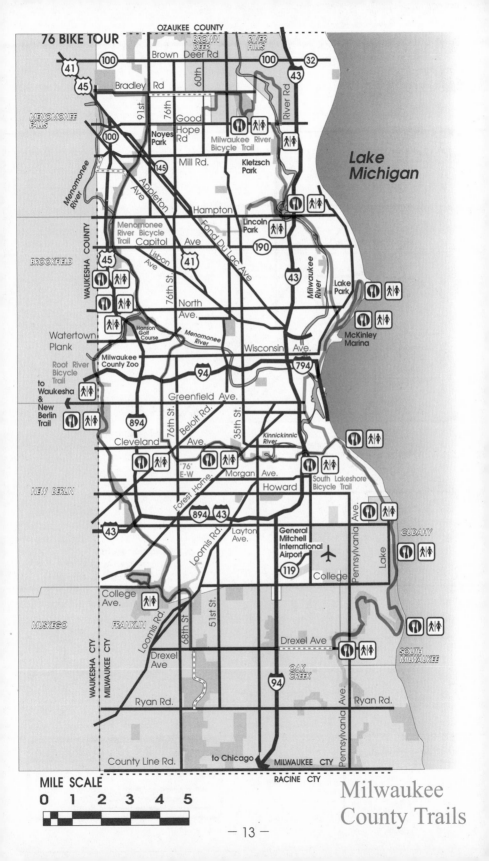

76 BIKE TOUR

Milwaukee
County Trails

Milwaukee County Trails

MENOMONEE RIVER BICYCLE TRAIL

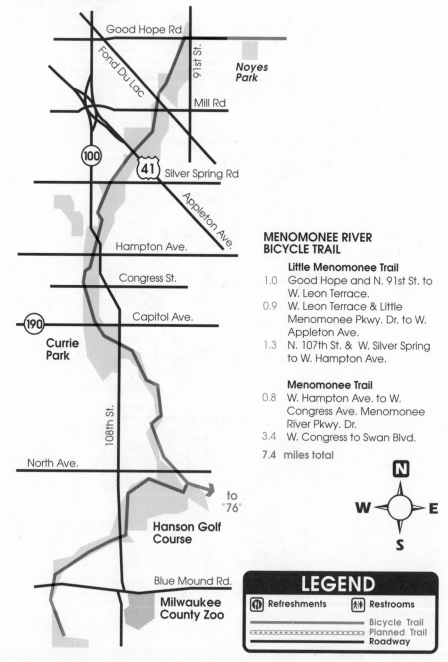

MENOMONEE RIVER BICYCLE TRAIL

Little Menomonee Trail

1.0 Good Hope and N. 91st St. to W. Leon Terrace.

0.9 W. Leon Terrace & Little Menomonee Pkwy. Dr. to W. Appleton Ave.

1.3 N. 107th St. & W. Silver Spring to W. Hampton Ave.

Menomonee Trail

0.8 W. Hampton Ave. to W. Congress Ave. Menomonee River Pkwy. Dr.

3.4 W. Congress to Swan Blvd.

7.4 miles total

LEGEND

| | Refreshments | | Restrooms |

Bicycle Trail
Planned Trail
Roadway

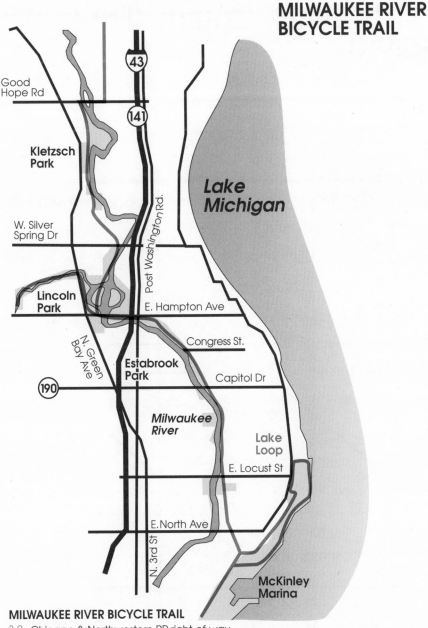

MILWAUKEE RIVER BICYCLE TRAIL

Good Hope Rd

Kletzsch Park

W. Silver Spring Dr

Lincoln Park

Estabrook Park

Milwaukee River

Lake Michigan

E. Hampton Ave

Congress St.

Capitol Dr

Lake Loop

E. Locust St

E. North Ave

McKinley Marina

Post Washington Rd.

N. Green Bay Ave

N. 3rd St

MILWAUKEE RIVER BICYCLE TRAIL

3.2   Chicago & Northwestern RR right-of-way.

Estabrook Trail

1.5   Estabrook Park & C&NWRR r-o-w to Hampton Ave. & N. Port Washington Rd.

Lincoln Park Trail.

1.7   Hampton Ave. & N. Port Washington Rd. to W. Silver Spring Dr. & Milwaukee River Pkwy. Dr.

0.9   W. Silver Spring Dr. & Milwaukee River Pkwy. Dr. to W. Bender Rd. & Milwaukee River Pkwy. Dr.

Kletzsch Park Trail

1.3   W. Bender Rd. and Milwaukee River Pkwy. Dr. to W. Good Hope Rd. & Milwaukee River Pkwy. Dr.

8.6 miles total

Milwaukee County Trails

Milwaukee County Trails

ROOT RIVER BICYCLE TRAIL

Root River Pkwy. Dr. & W. Layton Ave. to Root River Pkwy. Dr. & Loomis Rd. (includes 3.3 mile Whitnall Park loop).

7.7 miles total

ROOT RIVER BICYCLE TRAIL

9.1 Loomis Rd. at 68th St. to 10000 W. Layton Ave.

1.9 W. Layton Ave. to 11600 W. Morgan Ave.

3.3 W. Morgan Ave. to 12000 W. Greenfield Ave.

14.3 miles total

SOUTH LAKEFRONT BICYCLE TRAIL

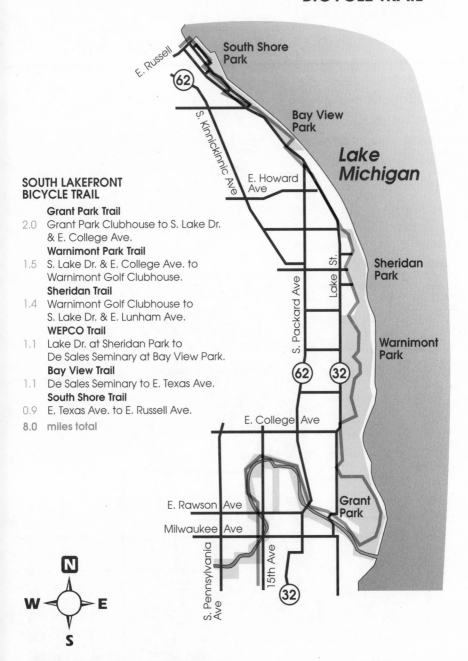

SOUTH LAKEFRONT BICYCLE TRAIL

South Shore Park

Bay View Park

Lake Michigan

E. Russell

S. Kinnickinnic Ave

E. Howard Ave

S. Packard Ave

Lake St.

Sheridan Park

Warnimont Park

E. College Ave

E. Rawson Ave

Milwaukee Ave

S. Pennsylvania Ave

15th Ave

Grant Park

**SOUTH LAKEFRONT
BICYCLE TRAIL**

Grant Park Trail
2.0   Grant Park Clubhouse to S. Lake Dr. & E. College Ave.
Warnimont Park Trail
1.5   S. Lake Dr. & E. College Ave. to Warnimont Golf Clubhouse.
Sheridan Trail
1.4   Warnimont Golf Clubhouse to S. Lake Dr. & E. Lunham Ave.
WEPCO Trail
1.1   Lake Dr. at Sheridan Park to De Sales Seminary at Bay View Park.
Bay View Trail
1.1   De Sales Seminary to E. Texas Ave.
South Shore Trail
0.9   E. Texas Ave. to E. Russell Ave.

8.0   miles total

N
W   E
S

LEGEND

Refreshments   Restrooms

———— Bicycle Trail
·········· Planned Trail
———— Roadway

Milwaukee
County Trails

Racine County Trails

Trail Length	20 miles (plus over 100 miles of designated bikeways)
Surface	Crushed limestone
Uses	Bicycling, hiking, x-c skiing
Location & Setting	Varies from the urban city of Racine, to smaller communities such as Burlington and Waterford, to open areas and agricultural.
Information	Racine County Visitors Bureau 800/272-2463 345 Main Street, Racine, WI 53403 Racine County Public Works 414/886-8440 14200 Washington Ave., Sturtevant, WI 53177
County	Racine

Colonel Heg Memorial Park - contains a museum highlighting the unique heritage of early Norwegian settlers. It is the site of "Heritage Days" held in June each year. The park offers picnic areas and a comfort station.

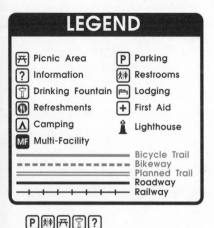

LEGEND

🏕 Picnic Area	🅿 Parking
❓ Information	🚻 Restrooms
⛲ Drinking Fountain	🛏 Lodging
🍴 Refreshments	✚ First Aid
⛺ Camping	⚓ Lighthouse
MF Multi-Facility	

─────── Bicycle Trail
- - - - - - - Bikeway
═══════ Planned Trail
━━━━━━━ Roadway
┼┼┼┼┼┼┼ Railway

🅿 🚻 🏕 ⛲ ❓
MF ● ● ● ●

EMERGENCY ASSISTANCE   **-DIAL 911**
Racine - St. Luke's Hospital   -414/636-2011
Racine - St. Mary's Medical Ctr. -414/636-4011

Racine County Trails

North Shore	3 miles
M.R.K.	5 miles
Racine Sturtevant	3 miles
Burlington	4 miles
Waterford/Wind Lake	4 miles
Norway	1.2 miles

Cliffside Park - offers a winding nature trail through a wooded ravine, children's play area, and reservable picnic areas with tables and grills. The park has family campsites, comfort stations, and a sanitary station for RV campers.

Racine Harbor Park - located on Lake Michigan with easy access to downtown Racine. There is an elevated deck providing a great view of Lake Michigan and points of interest along the shoreline.

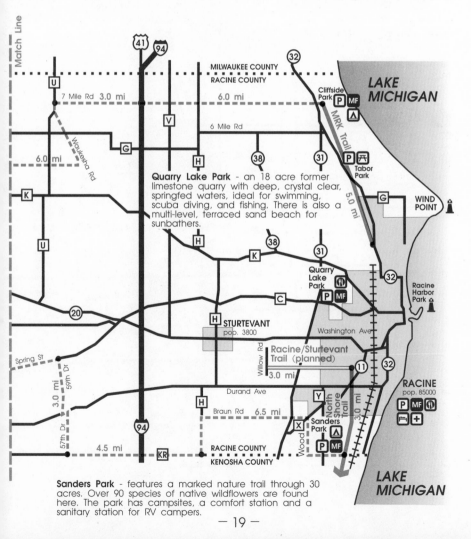

Quarry Lake Park - an 18 acre former limestone quarry with deep, crystal clear, springfed waters, ideal for swimming, scuba diving, and fishing. There is also a multi-level, terraced sand beach for sunbathers.

Sanders Park - features a marked nature trail through 30 acres. Over 90 species of native wildflowers are found here. The park has campsites, a comfort station and a sanitary station for RV campers.

Kenosha County Trails

Trail Length	7.5 miles (plus 6.5 miles of connecting streets)
Surface	Crushed limestone (other than streets)
Uses	Bicycling, hiking, x-c skiing
Location & Setting	Open areas, sparse woods, urban streets. The Kenosha County Bike Trail is a marked trail starting at the Illinois border connected with streets to and north along the lakefront and then by trail again to the Racine County line.
Information	Kenosha County Parks 414/857-1869 P.O. Box 549., Bristol, WI 53104
County	Kenosha

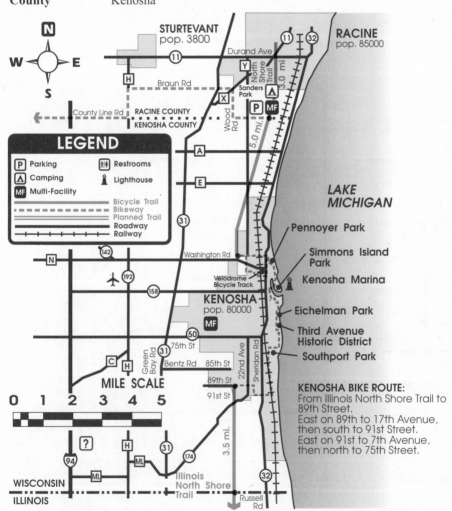

LEGEND

P Parking
A Camping
MF Multi-Facility
Restrooms
Lighthouse

Bicycle Trail
Bikeway
Planned Trail
Roadway
Railway

STURTEVANT pop. 3800
Durand Ave
RACINE pop. 85000
North Shore Trail
3.0 mi.
Braun Rd
Sanders Park
County Line Rd
RACINE COUNTY
KENOSHA COUNTY
Wood Rd
5.0 mi.

LAKE MICHIGAN

Pennoyer Park
Simmons Island Park
Kenosha Marina
Velodrome Bicycle Track
KENOSHA pop. 80000
Eichelman Park
Third Avenue Historic District
Southport Park

Washington Rd
Green Bay Rd
75th St
Bentz Rd 85th St
89th St
91st St
Sheridan Rd
22nd Ave

MILE SCALE
0 1 2 3 4 5

WISCONSIN
ILLINOIS
Illinois North Shore Trail
Russell Rd
3.5 mi.

KENOSHA BIKE ROUTE:
From Illinois North Shore Trail to 89th Street.
East on 89th to 17th Avenue, then south to 91st Street.
East on 91st to 7th Avenue, then north to 75th Street.

Waukesha County Overview

Information Waukesha County Parks & Recreation - 414/548-7801
500 Riverview Ave., Waukesha, WI 54935

Waukesha Visitors Bureau - 800/366-1961

WAUKESHA BIKEWAY CONNECTION TO GLACIAL DRUMLIN TRAIL

From **The New Berlin Trail,
south on Springdale Rd-
.7 miles to Broadway**

West on Broadway-
1.3 miles to Oakland Ave. (south)

South on Oakland Ave.-
1 block to College Ave. (west).

West on College Ave. to **Fox River
Sanctuary (bike trail)**-1.2 miles
**Parking and restrooms
available at Sanctuary.**

Waukesha County, located in southeast
Wisconsin and just west of Milwaukee, offers a
wide variety of recreational activities. There are
numerous biking, cross-country skiing, hiking and
snowmobiling trails in the state and county
parks. The county has 77 lakes, 10 campgrounds,
and 17 golf courses, all open to the public.

P **Denotes Parking**

New Berlin Recreational Trail

Trail Length	6 miles
Surface	Limestone screenings
Uses	Bicycling, x-c skiing, hiking
Location & Setting	The New Berlin Recreational Trail is located in southeastern Wisconsin in Waukesha County. The eastern trailhead is in Greenfield Park, which connects to Milwaukee County's extensive trail system. The trail proceeds west to Springdale Road in the city of Waukesha. It is built on the Wisconsin Electric Power Co. right-of-way.
Information	Waukesha County Parks & Recreation 414/548-7801 500 Riverview Ave., Waukesha, WI 54935 Waukesha Visitors Bureau 800/366-1961
County	Waukesha

MINOOKA PARK HIKING TRAIL

Surface	-	Natural-groomed, wood chipped
Trail Length	-	6.0 miles
Uses	-	X-C Skiing, hiking
Setting	-	Wooded, hilly, open fields

Minooka Park, part of the Waukesha County Park system, is located south of the New Berlin Trail on Racine Ave. (CTH Y). Facilities and activities include: parking, restrooms, water, picnicking, swimming, hiking, X-C skiing and sledding. Concessions are available at the beach house during the swimming season.

LEGEND

P Parking	**⊼** Picnic Area
? Information	**⚇** Restrooms
⛲ Drinking Fountain	**C** Telephone
MF Multi-Facility	

——————— Bicycle Trail
- - - - - - - Bikeway
━━━━━━━ Roadway
+-+-+-+-+ Railway

Lake Country Recreation Trail

Trail Length	8 miles
Surface	Crushed limestone
Uses	Bicycling, x-c skiing, hiking/jogging
Location & Setting	The Lake Country Recreation Trail is located in southeastern Wisconsin. The trail stretches between the Landsberg Center trailhead, just north of I-94 on Golf Road, and Cushing Park in the city of Delafield. The Lake Country Trail utilizes the Wisconsin Electric Power Company's right-of-way which was also the former Milwaukee-Watertown Interurban Railway.
Information	Waukesha County Park Office 414/548-7801 1320 Pewaukee Road, Room 230 Waukesha, WI 53188
County	Waukesha

The Lake Country Trail is accessible at all road crossings and at Naga-Waukee Park. Trail information, parking, shelter, and water are available at the Landsberg Center trailhead next to the Country Inn. Near the west end of the trail near the town of Delafield is a selection of food shops and other facilities

The trail has access to the Naga-Waukee park just west of Hwy. 83. Facilities include drinking water, concessions, picnicking, camping, swimming, boating, and field sports. There is a park entrance fee for vehicles.

The trail shares the road with vehicles for short distances at Hwy. SS and Oakton Road and at Wells Street in the city of Delafield.

LEGEND

- P Parking
- A Camping
- Drinking Fountain
- Picnic Area
- Shelter
- ▬▬▬ Bicycle Trail
- ▬ ▬ ▬ Bikeway
- ▬▬▬ Roadway

Bugline Trail

Trail Length	12.2 miles
Surface	Crushed limestone
Uses	Bicycling, x-c skiing, snowmobiling, hiking, horseback riding
Location & Setting	The Bugline Recreational Trail is located in Waukesha County in southwestern Wisconsin. The eastern trailhead is off Appleton Avenue just north of Hwy. 175 in Menomonee Falls. The trail proceeds west to the town of Merton on an old railroad right-of-way.
Information	Waukesha County Park Office 414/548-7801 500 Riverview Ave., Waukesha, WI 54935 Waukesha Visitors Bureau 800/366-1961
County	Waukesha

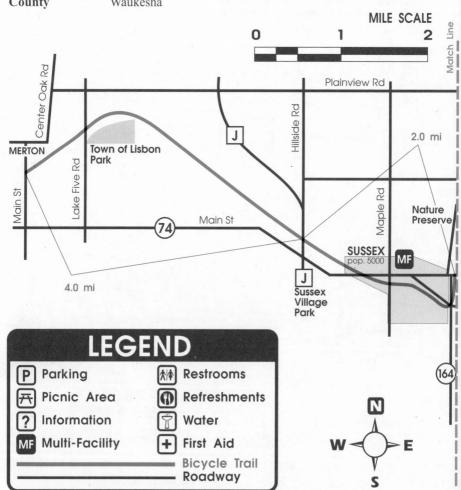

Menomonee Park, part of the Waukesha County Park System, is a trailhead as well a recreation site along the Bugline Trail. Facilities and activities include: parking, restrooms, water, picnicking, camping, swimming, hiking, fishing, X-C skiing, and sledding. Concessions are available at the beach house during the swimming season.

MENOMONEE PARK HIKING TRAIL

Trail Length - 4.5 miles
Surface - Natural-groomed, wood chipped
Uses - Hiking, X-C Skiing
Setting - Wooded, rolling, wetlands

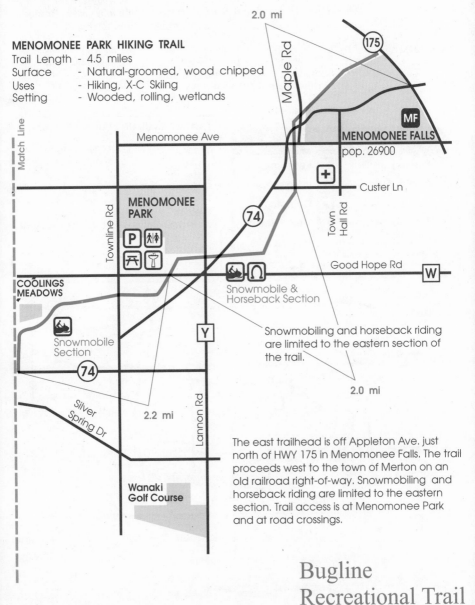

Snowmobiling and horseback riding are limited to the eastern section of the trail.

The east trailhead is off Appleton Ave. just north of HWY 175 in Menomonee Falls. The trail proceeds west to the town of Merton on an old railroad right-of-way. Snowmobiling and horseback riding are limited to the eastern section. Trail access is at Menomonee Park and at road crossings.

Bugline
Recreational Trail

Glacial Drumlin State Trail
Western Section

Trail Length	47.2 miles	
Surface	Limestone screenings (7 miles paved Waukesha to Wales)	
Uses	Bicycling, x-c skiing, snowmobiling, hiking	
Location & Setting	The Glacial Drumlin State Park Trail is located in southern Wisconsin and runs from Waukesha (by the Fox River Sanctuary) to Cottage Grove, 11 miles east of Madison. It was built on abandoned Chicago and Northwestern rail line and passes through many small communities, prairie remnants, and farmland.	
Information	Glacial Drumlin State Trail-East	414/646-3025
	Glacial Drumlin State Trail-West	414/648-8774
	Waukesha County Chamber of Commerce	414/542-4249
	Lake Mills Chamber of Commerce	414/648-3585
Counties	Waukesha, Jefferson, Dane	

LEGEND

P	Parking	👫	Restrooms
🚻	Picnic Area	?	Information
🏪	Refreshments	🅰	Camping
🔧	Bicycle Service	MF	Multi-Facility

━━━ Bicycle Trail
▬ ▬ ▬ Bikeway
━━━ Roadway

GLACIAL DRUMLIN STATE PARK TRAIL ROUTE SLIP:

	SEGMENT	TOTAL
Waukesha		
Wales	6.5	6.5
Dousman	4.5	11.0
Sullivan	6.6	17.6
Helenville	5.9	23.5
Switzke Rd.	2.1	25.6
East-West Connection	*4.0 mi. bikeway*	
Lake Mills	5.9	31.5
London	5.8	37.3
Deerfield	3.2	40.5
Cottage Grove	6.7	47.2

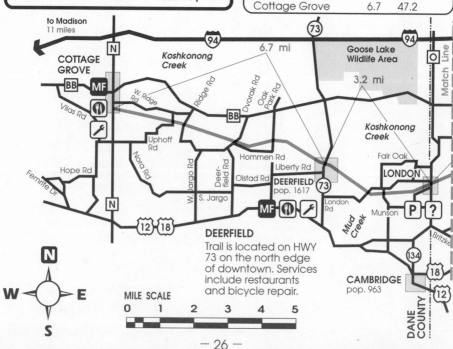

DEERFIELD
Trail is located on HWY 73 on the north edge of downtown. Services include restaurants and bicycle repair.

MILE SCALE
0 1 2 3 4 5

Drumlins are the long hills left behind by melting glaciers thousands of years ago. The Glacial Drumlin Trail comes within a few miles of the Aztalan State Park, Lapham Peak, and the southern unit of Kettle Moraine State Forest.

GLACIAL DRUMLIN STATE TRAIL OVERVIEW

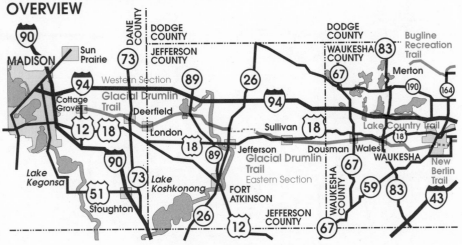

EAST-WEST TRAIL CONNECTION

There is a 4 mile gap in the trail between Helenville and Jefferson requiring the use of low traffic road connections. Take Switzke Road .5 mile north to Marsh Road, then 1.7 miles west to Hwy. Y, then south on Y to Junction Road. Take Junction Road 1.7 miles west to Hwy 26 from where the trail continues west.

Portions of the trail between county "O" and road "S" may be closed at times during the summer for herbicide application.

LAKE MILLS

HWY 89 to CTH "A" train depot station. Parking at trail. Services include restaurants and village parks with water & restrooms.

Glacial Drumlin St. Trail
Western Section

Glacial Drumlin State Trail
Eastern Section

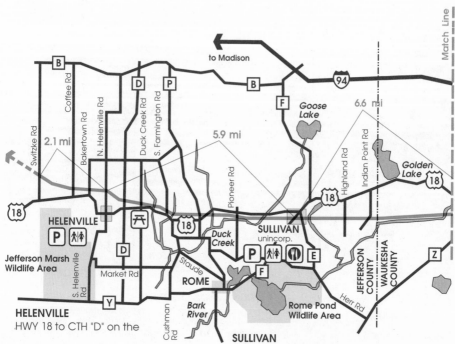

to Madison

Match Line

HELENVILLE
HWY 18 to CTH "D" on the

MILE SCALE

0 1 2 3 4 5

N
W — **E**
S

LEGEND

P	Parking	🚻	Restrooms
🏕	Picnic Area	?	Information
🏪	Refreshments	A	Camping
🔧	Bicycle Service	MF	Multi-Facility

━━━ Bicycle Trail
- - - - - Bikeway
━━━ Roadway

SULLIVAN
West on HWY 18 from CTH "F" to Palmyra St. to trail crossing. Parking & restrooms adjacent to trail on Palmyra St. Facilities include restaurant, village park, picnicking.

DOUSMAN
HWY 18 west of HWY 67 to Main St. South on Main St. 3/4 mile to trail crossing. Parking adjacent to trail. Services include restaurant, village park next to trail with water & restrooms.

GLACIAL DRUMLIN STATE PARK TRAIL ROUTE SLIP:

Waukesha	SEGMENT	TOTAL
Wales	6.5	6.5
Dousman	4.5	11.0
Sullivan	6.6	17.6
Helenville	5.9	23.5
Switzke Rd.	2.1	25.6
East-West Connection	*4.0 mi. bikeway*	
Lake Mills	5.9	31.5
London	5.8	37.3
Deerfield	3.2	40.5
Cottage Grove	6.7	47.2

You can camp at the Kettle Moraine and Lake Kegonsa State Parks, and at the Nagawicka County Park. The trail crosses the Rock and the Crawfish rivers. Many area lakes provide fishing and boating.

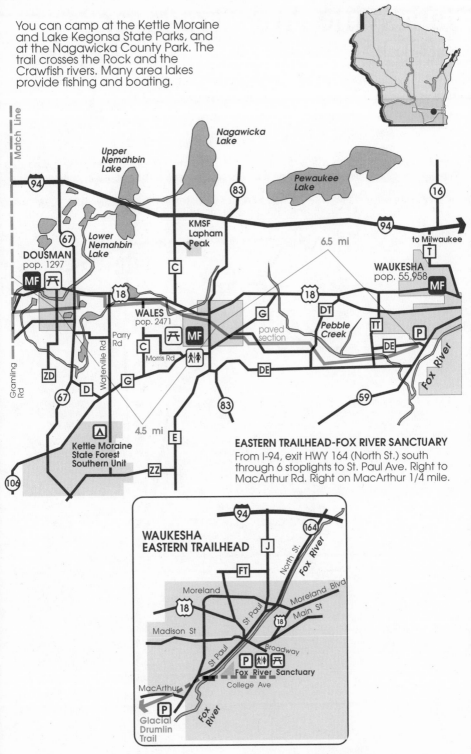

EASTERN TRAILHEAD-FOX RIVER SANCTUARY
From I-94, exit HWY 164 (North St.) south through 6 stoplights to St. Paul Ave. Right to MacArthur Rd. Right on MacArthur 1/4 mile.

Janesville Area Trails

Trail Length	10 miles (plus 25 miles of designated bikeways)
Surface	Paved, rolled gravel (Rock River Parkway)
Uses	Bicycling, in-line skating, x-c skiing, jogging
Location & Setting	Janesville is located in southeastern Wisconsin. The economy base is manufacturing and agriculture. The setting is urban and parkways.
Information	Janesville Leisure Services Division 608/755-3025 17 North Franklin Street, Janesville, WI 53535
County	Rock

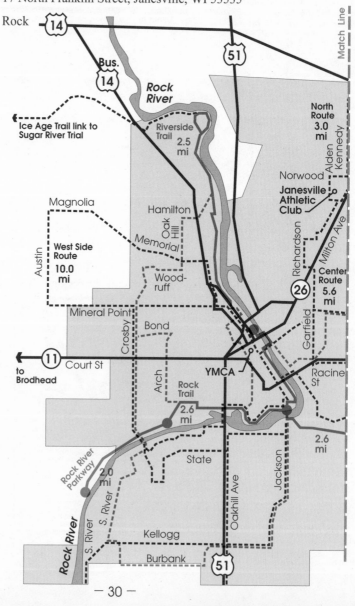

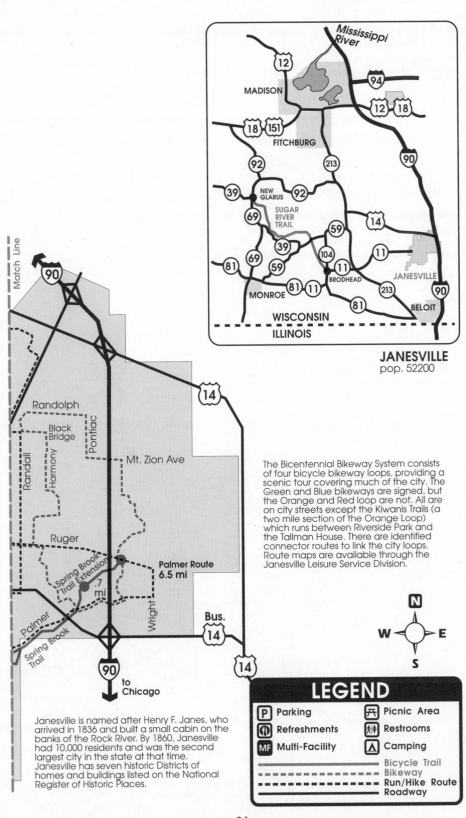

Mississippi River

MADISON

FITCHBURG

NEW GLARUS

SUGAR RIVER TRAIL

MONROE

BRODHEAD

JANESVILLE

BELOIT

WISCONSIN

ILLINOIS

JANESVILLE
pop. 52200

Match Line

90

14

Randolph

Black Bridge

Pontiac

Mt. Zion Ave

Randall

Harmony

Ruger

Spring Brook Trail Extension

.7 mi

Palmer Route
6.5 mi

Wright

Palmer

Spring Brook Trail

90

to Chicago

Bus. 14

14

The Bicentennial Bikeway System consists of four bicycle bikeway loops, providing a scenic tour covering much of the city. The Green and Blue bikeways are signed, but the Orange and Red loop are not. All are on city streets except the Kiwanis Trails (a two mile section of the Orange Loop) which runs between Riverside Park and the Tallman House. There are identified connector routes to link the city loops. Route maps are available through the Janesville Leisure Service Division.

N
W   E
S

Janesville is named after Henry F. Janes, who arrived in 1836 and built a small cabin on the banks of the Rock River. By 1860, Janesville had 10,000 residents and was the second largest city in the state at that time. Janesville has seven historic Districts of homes and buildings listed on the National Register of Historic Places.

LEGEND

P	Parking	🏕	Picnic Area
🛈	Refreshments	🚻	Restrooms
MF	Multi-Facility	⛺	Camping

Bicycle Trail
Bikeway
Run/Hike Route
Roadway

Madison Area Trails & Bikeways

Trail Length	Off street trails - 20 miles Striped bike lanes - 13 miles Signed street routes - over 100 miles
Surface	Asphalt & street lanes
Uses	Bicycling, in-line skating, jogging, x-c skiing
Location & Setting	Madison is a city of 92,000 in south central Wisconsin and is the State Capital. The setting is urban and parks.
Information	Greater Madison Visitors Bureau 800/373-6376 615 East Washington Avenue Madison, WI 53703
County	Dane

Madison is a bicycling town where bicycles outnumber autos. Bicyclists are assisted in their travel around central Madison by special bicycle related facilities separate bicycle paths and lanes. Numerous bike racks are located throughout the area.

MADISON
pop. 92000

See following pages for city trails and bikeways

Match Line

19

113

M

12

Lake Mendota

M

14

S

M

12 14

Lake Wingra

18

14 151

12 18

D

M

PD

PD

Planned Capital City State Trail

Military Ridge State Park Trail

151

14

VERONA

PB

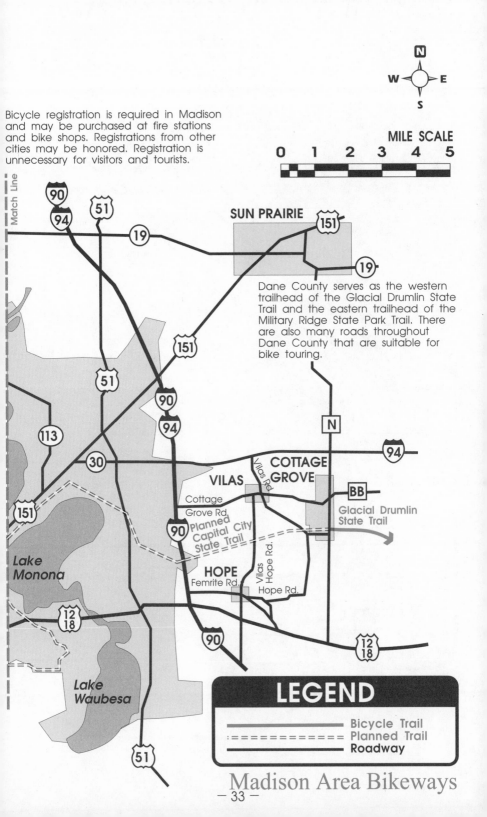

Bicycle registration is required in Madison and may be purchased at fire stations and bike shops. Registrations from other cities may be honored. Registration is unnecessary for visitors and tourists.

Match Line

MILE SCALE

0 1 2 3 4 5

SUN PRAIRIE

Dane County serves as the western trailhead of the Glacial Drumlin State Trail and the eastern trailhead of the Military Ridge State Park Trail. There are also many roads throughout Dane County that are suitable for bike touring.

COTTAGE GROVE

VILAS

Vilas Rd.

BB

Cottage Grove Rd.

Glacial Drumlin State Trail

Planned City Capital City State Trail

Lake Monona

HOPE
Femrite Rd.

Vilas Hope Rd.

Hope Rd.

Lake Waubesa

LEGEND

━━━━━━	Bicycle Trail
===========	Planned Trail
━━━━━━	Roadway

Madison Area Bikeways

Madison Area Trails & Bikewys

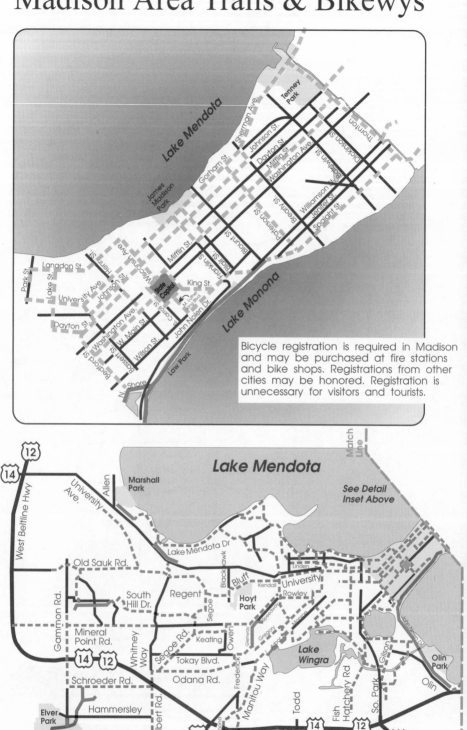

Bicycle registration is required in Madison and may be purchased at fire stations and bike shops. Registrations from other cities may be honored. Registration is unnecessary for visitors and tourists.

Bicycles are permitted on all streets in Madison, except for limited access highways such as the Beltline. What streets a bicyclist chooses to use will depend upon their skill and confidence levels, as well as their origin and destination. The city is attempting to make all streets friendly for bicyclists.

Conditions on the roads in Madison can vary depending on the time of day, the day of the week and the season. Increased congestion during rush hours or construction may call for extra caution. Bicyclists should be prepared to make their own evaluation of traffic and road conditions, and plan routes appropriate to their riding skills. Each bicyclist assumes the risks encountered and is advised to use good judgment and obey traffic laws on all routes, regardless of their designation.

In Wisconsin, the bicycle is considered a vehicle, subject to the same vehicle code as autos. Keep these safety tips in mind:
All bikes must be registered in Madison.
Have a front light and rear deflector at night.
Do not ride on sidewalks in business areas.
Yield to pedestrians and cross traffic.
Do not park bikes against trees.
Do not pass between buses on the State St. Mall
Always lock your bike.

LEGEND

Bicycle Trail
Bikeway
Roadway

MILE SCALE

0   1   2

Madison Area Bikeways

Sugar River State Park Trail

Trail Length	23.5 miles
Surface	Crushed limestone
Uses	Bicycling, hiking, x-c skiing, snowmobiling
Location & Setting	The Sugar River State Park trail runs for 23.5 miles between New Glarus (northwest trailhead) and Brodhead (southeast trailhead) in south central Wisconsin. It passes through gently rolling hills, quarries, woodlands, a covered bridge and the Albany Wildlife Refuge.
Information	Trail Manager, Sugar River State Park Trail 608/527-2334 P.O. Box 781, New Glarus, WI 53574
County	Green

TRAIL ADMISSION FEES
Trail passes are required for bikers 18 years old and older. Fees vary as to whether daily or seasonal. Passes are good on all Wisconsin State Trails. Passes are available at the trail headquarters in New Glarus, at New Glarus Woods State Park and at outlets in communities along the trail.

New Glarus, known as "Little Switzerland", was founded in 1845 by Swiss immigrants from Glarus, Switzerland. The trail headquarters, located here in a former Milwaukee Road depot, offers nature and history displays and a driver-only shuttle service.

New Glarus Events:
Late June   - Heidi Drama; Heidi Craft & Food Fair
Late June   - Little Switzerland Festival
Early August - Volksfest (Swiss Independence Day)
              - Wilhelm Tell Drama in English & German

NEW GLARUS

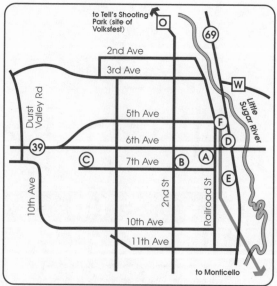

Approximate distances from major cities:

Madison to New Glarus - 22 miles

Milwaukee to New Glarus - 100 miles

Chicago to Brodhead - 130 miles

NEW GLARUS ATTRACTIONS

Ⓐ Information Booth

Ⓑ Chalet of the Golden Fleece

Ⓒ Swiss Historical Village

Ⓓ Historical Marker (Hwy 69)

Ⓔ Floral Clock

Ⓕ Sugar River State Trail Headquarters

There are parking and picnic facilities in all the communities along the trail, and at five other spots as well. Both New Glarus and Brodhead have public swimming pools. The local communities hold numerous festivals throughout the summer, including:

Albany – Yesteryear Day & Country/Bluegrass Music Festival
Monticello – Summerfest
New Glarus – Wilhelm Tell Drama, Heidi Festival, & Volkfest

HISTORY

The first inhabitants were Sauk and Fox Indians, followed by the Winnebagos. The Winnebagos were forced out of the area after the Black Hawk War in 1832. Settlers began arriving in 1845. The railroad began operation in 1880, and ceased in 1972.

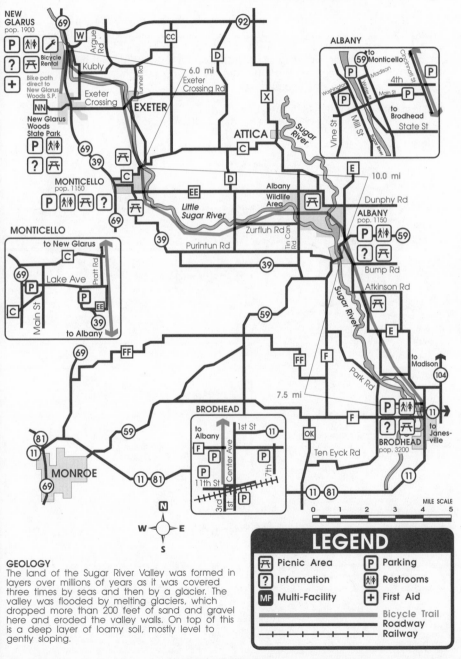

GEOLOGY

The land of the Sugar River Valley was formed in layers over millions of years as it was covered three times by seas and then by a glacier. The valley was flooded by melting glaciers, which dropped more than 200 feet of sand and gravel here and eroded the valley walls. On top of this is a deep layer of loamy soil, mostly level to gently sloping.

Military Ridge State Park Trail

Trail Length	39.6 miles
Surface	Crushed limestone
Uses	Bicycling, x-c skiing, snowmobiling, hiking
Location & Setting	The Military Ridge State Park Trail runs from Verona west to Dodgeville, passing through the communities of Mt. Horeb, Blue Mounds, Barneveld, and Ridgeway. The trail follows the abandoned Chicago and Northwestern railway line and includes 48 bridges. The setting consists of farmland, prairie, wooded areas, and small communities.
Information	Governor Dodge State Park 608/935-2315 4175 State Road 23, Dodgeville, WI 53533
Counties	Dane, Iowa

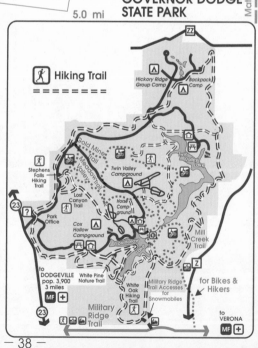

DODGEVILLE
Located at the gateway to the Uplands; a geographic maze of rolling farmlands, wooded valleys and rugged sandstone bluffs. Wildlife in the area includes fox, turkeys, deer and coyotes.

GOVERNOR DODGE STATE PARK
Located 3 miles north of Dodgeville on State Hwy 23. It is the 2nd largest state park in Wisconsin. The terrain in the park is rugged and varies from steep hills and sandstone bluffs to deep lush valleys. Activities include hiking, horseback riding, swimming, picnicking, and camping. There is an admission fee.

CAVE OF THE MOUNDS
Located 3 miles west of Mt. Horeb just off US Hwys. 18/151. A guided tour of the Cave takes you past a varied collection of stalactites, stalagmites, columns and other formations. There are park-like grounds with picnic areas, rock gardens and an outdoor amphitheater.

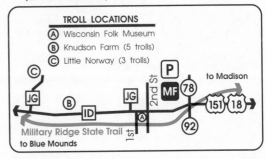

MOUNT HOREB
(LITTLE NORWAY)

TROLL LOCATIONS
A Wisconsin Folk Museum
B Knudson Farm (5 trolls)
C Little Norway (3 trolls)

Military Ridge State Trail
to Blue Mounds
to Madison

LITTLE NORWAY
Located 3 miles west of Mt. Horeb among the rolling hills of Blue Mounds. It is known as the "Valley of the Elves". The guides will tour you through buildings containing the largest privately owned collection of Norwegian antiques in the country.

MOUNT HOREB
The "Troll" capital of the world. The area is rocky with abrupt hills and narrow, winding valleys. Attractions include Cave of the Mounds, Little Norway, several small museums and a number of tourist shops.

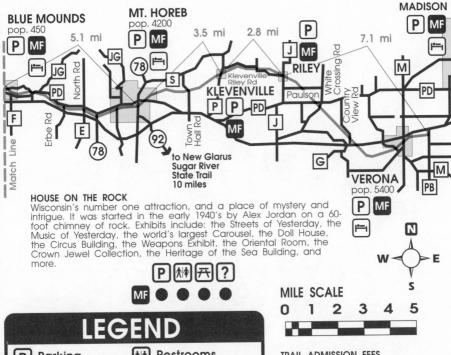

HOUSE ON THE ROCK
Wisconsin's number one attraction, and a place of mystery and intrigue. It was started in the early 1940's by Alex Jordan on a 60-foot chimney of rock. Exhibits include: the Streets of Yesterday, the Music of Yesterday, the world's largest Carousel, the Doll House, the Circus Building, the Weapons Exhibit, the Oriental Room, the Crown Jewel Collection, the Heritage of the Sea Building, and more.

LEGEND

P	Parking		🏃	Restrooms
?	Information		🎋	Picnic Area
A	Camping		🛏	Lodging
🍴	Refreshments		+	First Aid
MF	Multi-Facility			

— Bicycle Trail
--- Mountain Biking
— Roadway

MILE SCALE
0 1 2 3 4 5

TRAIL ADMISSION FEES
Trail passes are required for bikers 18 years old and older. Fees vary as to whether daily or seasonal. Passes are good on all Wisconsin State Trails.

SHUTTLE SERVICE: A driver will transport cyclists to a desired point along the Trail from Mt. Horeb and return your car to Mt. Horeb.

Military Ridge
State Park Trail

Cheese Country Recreational Trail
Pecatonica State Trail 🚴 ⛷ 🎿 🧲 🏂

Trail Length	Cheese Country - 47 miles Pecatonica - 10 miles (+7 miles planned)
Surface	Crushed stone
Uses	Bicycling, x-c skiing, snowmobiling, hiking, horseback riding, ATV.
Location & Setting	The Cheese Country and Pecatonica Trails are located in south- western Wisconsin, as close as six miles from Illinois and 40 miles from Iowa. The Cheese Country Trail parallels the Pecatonica River and is built on the abandoned Milwaukee Road railbed. The Pecatonica Trial connects the Cheese Country Trail at Calamine and proceeds westerly 10 miles to Belmont. The setting consists of farmland, prairie, small communities and wetlands.
Information	Lafayette County Zoning Administrator 608/776-4830 Ag Center, 627 N. Washington St. Darlington, WI 53530
	Pecatonica State Park Trail 608/523-4427
Counties	Green, Lafayette

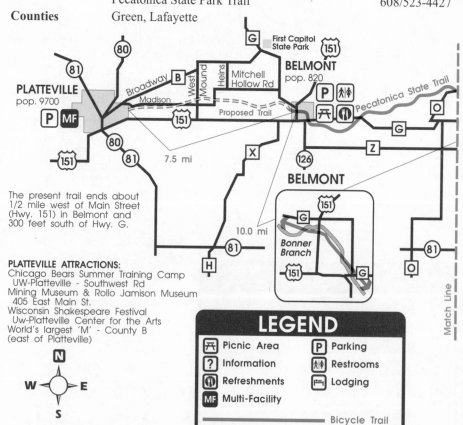

The present trail ends about
1/2 mile west of Main Street
(Hwy. 151) in Belmont and
300 feet south of Hwy. G.

PLATTEVILLE ATTRACTIONS:
Chicago Bears Summer Training Camp
 UW-Platteville - Southwest Rd
Mining Museum & Rollo Jamison Museum
 405 East Main St.
Wisconsin Shakespeare Festival
 Uw-Platteville Center for the Arts
World's largest 'M' - County B
(east of Platteville)

LEGEND

🛇	Picnic Area	P	Parking
?	Information	🚻	Restrooms
🍴	Refreshments	🛏	Lodging
MF	Multi-Facility		

———— Bicycle Trail
= = = = Proposed Trail
———— Roadway

MILE SCALE
0 1 2 3 4 5

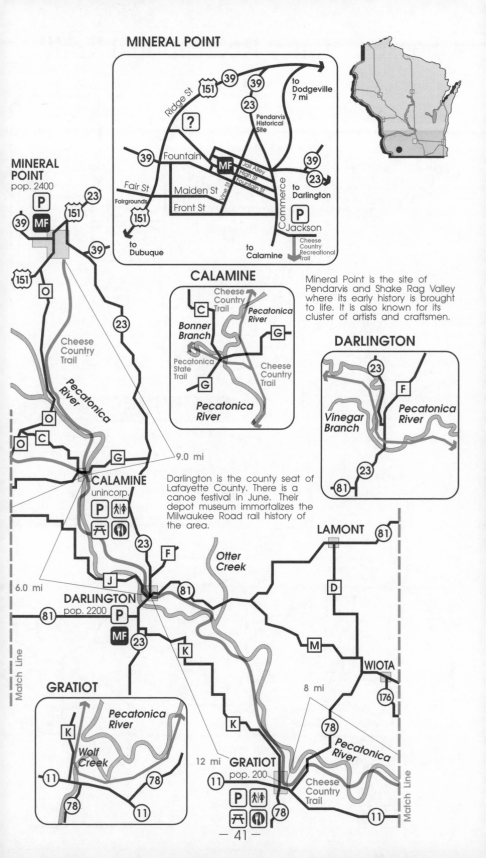

MINERAL POINT

MINERAL POINT
pop. 2400

to Dodgeville 7 mi

Pendarvis Historical Site

Ridge St

Fountain

Fair St

Maiden St

Front St

Fairgrounds

Jail Alley
High St
Fountain St

Vine St

Commerce

Jackson

to Darlington

to Calamine

to Dubuque

Cheese Country Recreational Trail

Mineral Point is the site of Pendarvis and Shake Rag Valley where its early history is brought to life. It is also known for its cluster of artists and craftsmen.

CALAMINE

Cheese Country Trail

Bonner Branch

Pecatonica River

Pecatonica State Trail

Cheese Country Trail

Pecatonica River

CALAMINE
unincorp.

DARLINGTON

Vinegar Branch

Pecatonica River

Darlington is the county seat of Lafayette County. There is a canoe festival in June. Their depot museum immortalizes the Milwaukee Road rail history of the area.

9.0 mi

Cheese Country Trail

Pecatonica River

6.0 mi

DARLINGTON
pop. 2200

Otter Creek

LAMONT

WIOTA

Match Line

GRATIOT

Pecatonica River

Wolf Creek

8 mi

Pecatonica River

12 mi

GRATIOT
pop. 200

Cheese Country Trail

Match Line

Cheese Country Recreational Trail

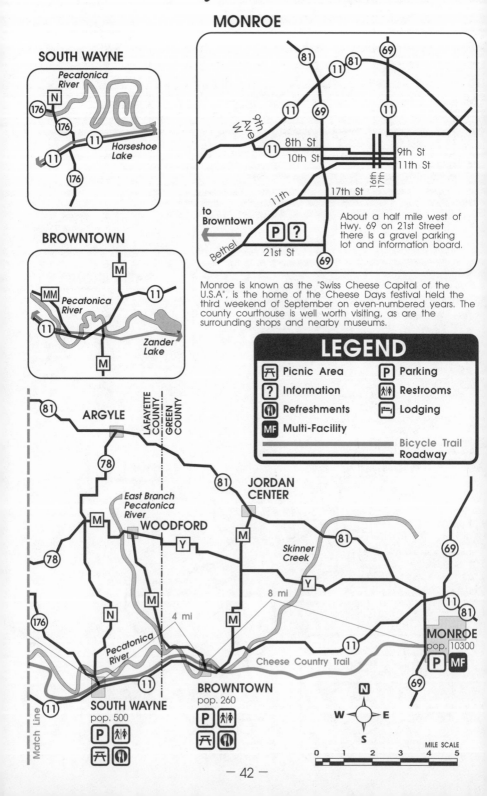

SOUTH WAYNE

Pecatonica River

N

176

176

11

Horseshoe Lake

11

176

MONROE

81

11 · 81

69

11

11 · 69

11

W 9th Ave

8th St

10th St

9th St

11th St

16th · 17th

17th St

11th

to Browntown

Bethel

P · ?

21st St

69

About a half mile west of Hwy. 69 on 21st Street there is a gravel parking lot and information board.

Monroe is known as the "Swiss Cheese Capital of the U.S.A", is the home of the Cheese Days festival held the third weekend of September on even-numbered years. The county courthouse is well worth visiting, as are the surrounding shops and nearby museums.

BROWNTOWN

M

MM · Pecatonica River

11

11

Zander Lake

M

LEGEND

🏕 Picnic Area   P Parking

? Information   🚻 Restrooms

🍴 Refreshments   🛏 Lodging

MF Multi-Facility

——— Bicycle Trail
——— Roadway

81

ARGYLE

LAFAYETTE COUNTY | GREEN COUNTY

78

East Branch Pecatonica River

M

WOODFORD

Y

81

JORDAN CENTER

M

Skinner Creek

81

69

78

N

M

Y

11 · 81

176

Pecatonica River

M

8 mi

4 mi

11

MONROE
pop. 10300

P · MF

11

Cheese Country Trail

11

SOUTH WAYNE
pop. 500

P · 🚻
🏕 · 🍴

BROWNTOWN
pop. 260

P · 🚻
🏕 · 🍴

69

Match Line

N
W · E
S

MILE SCALE

0 1 2 3 4 5

Pine River Trail

Trail Length	15 miles
Surface	Limestone screenings
Uses	Bicycling, x-c skiing, hiking
Location & Setting	The Pine River Trail is in southwest Wisconsin. The trail connects the communities of Richland Center and Lone Rock. It is built on abandoned railbed paralleling the western side of Hwy 14. The area is rural with popular tourist areas nearby such as House on the Rock and Governor Dodge State Park.
Information	Richland County Tourism Center 608/647-6148
Counties	Richland, Sauk

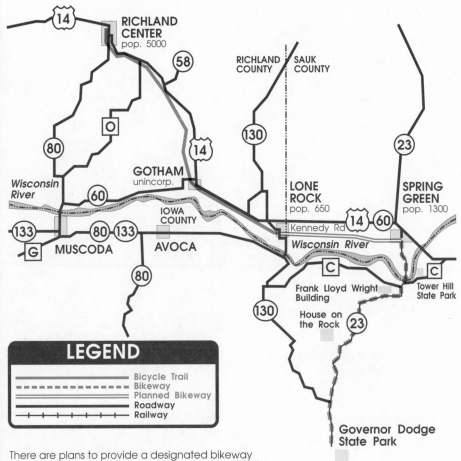

LEGEND

Bicycle Trail
Bikeway
Planned Bikeway
Roadway
Railway

There are plans to provide a designated bikeway along Kennedy Road Between Lone Rock and Spring Green. There currently exists a four foot designated bikeway on either side of Hwy. 23 out of Spring Green. This continues south on to House on the Rock and near Governor Dodge State Park.

Central Wisconsin Overview

63
94
Menomonie
53
Chippewa Falls
29
WAUSAU
29

Red Cedar Trail
EAU CLAIRE
13
51

63
10
Chippewa River Trl.
94
Fairchild
Marshfield
10

Mondovi
10

Buffalo River Trl.
53
Black River Falls
13
Wisconsin Rapids

93

Great River Trl.
94

Sparta
21

Onalaska
90

LA CROSSE
90
LaCrosse River Trl.
Omaha
94
16

14
Elroy-Sparta Trail
Wisconsin Dells
"400" Trl.

MINNESOTA
61

IOWA
12

14
Spring Green

61
14

WISCONSIN RIVER

MISSISSIPPI RIVER

ILLINOIS

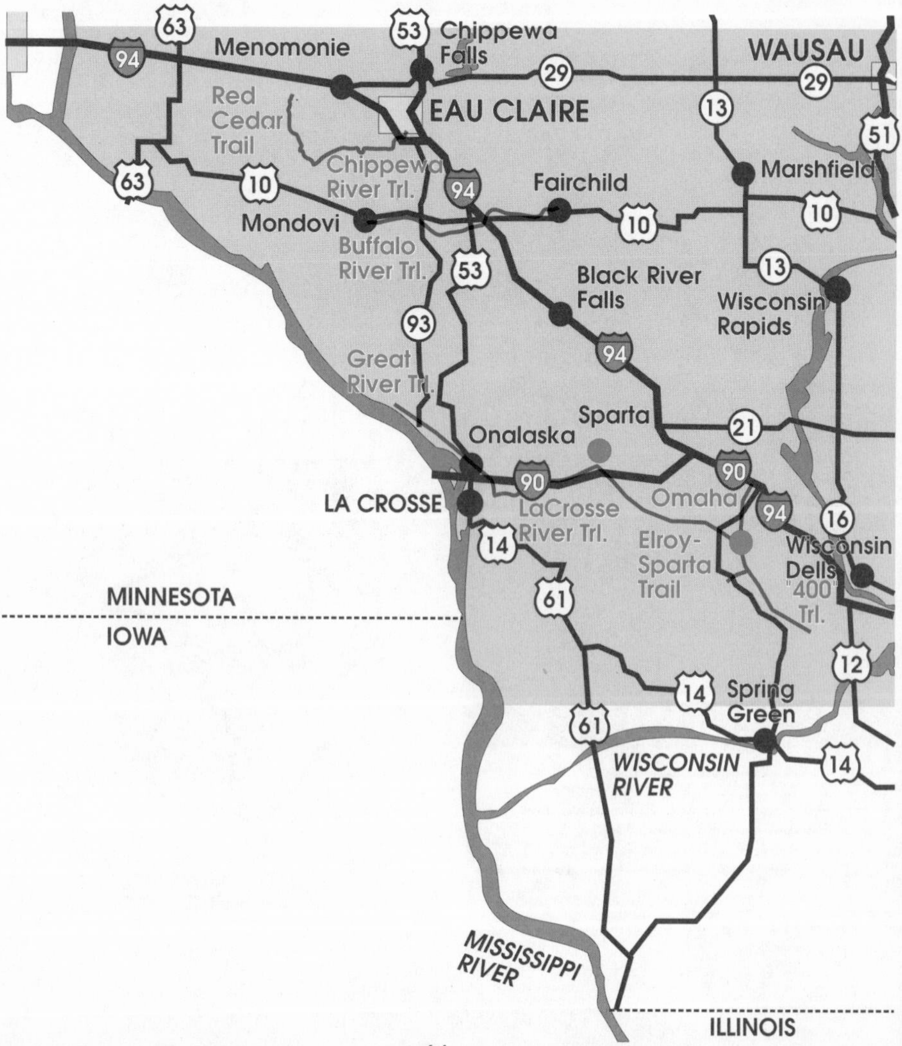

Peninsula S.P.

29

Mountain-Bay Trail

41 *Green Bay*

42 Door County

Sturgeon Bay

Stevens Point Green Circle

Shawano 29

57 42

Annapee St. Trl.

Algoma

GREEN BAY

45

CE Trail 41

43

Kewaunee

Hartman Creek S.P.

10

APPLETON

42

Wiowash Trail

10

21

OSHKOSH

151

MANITOWOC

51

LAKE WINNEBAGO

FOND DU LAC

Old Plank Road Trl.

SHEBOYGAN

Kohler

Wild Goose Trail

43

90

151

41

MADISON

94

MENOMONEE FALLS

Port Washington

94

MILWAUKEE

WAUKESHA

90

LAKE MICHIGAN

Door County Overview

Information   Door County Chamber of Commerce
P.O. Box 406, Sturgeon Bay, WI 54235

414/743-4456

Door County's varied landscape and roadways make it ideal for bicycle touring. The Backroad Bicycle Route is a 100 mile ride through fields and forests on country roads and byways. It links the small towns along both coasts. biking is at its best in the late spring and early fall.

Potawatomi State Park provides excellent biking and hiking trails and clean, sand beaches. The observation tower atop a limestone bluff offers a majestic view of Sawyer harbor.

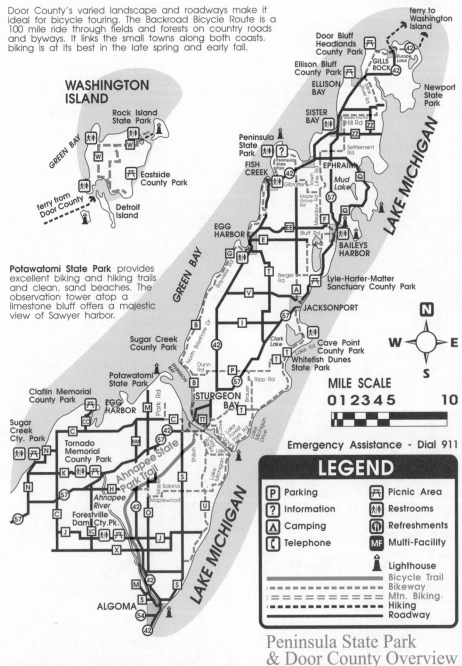

Emergency Assistance - Dial 911

MILE SCALE
0 1 2 3 4 5   10

LEGEND

P	Parking	🏕	Picnic Area
?	Information	🚻	Restrooms
A	Camping	🍴	Refreshments
C	Telephone	MF	Multi-Facility

Lighthouse
Bicycle Trail
Bikeway
Mtn. Biking
Hiking
Roadway

Peninsula State Park
& Door County Overview

Peninsula State Park

Trail Length	5 miles (plus 7 miles of Mtn. bikng trail)
Surface	Limestone screenings (Mtn. biking trail is unsurfaced)
Uses	Bicycling, x-c skiing, hiking
Location & Setting	The Peninsula State Park is located on the Green Bay side in upper Door County. The park has 3,763 acres of forest, dolomite cliffs, marsh, and meadows.
Information	Peninsula State Park 414/868-3258 Box 218, Fish Creek, WI 54212
County	Door

The Eagle Bluff Lighthouse is on the National Register of Historic Places. Located in Peninsula State Park between Fish Creek and Ephraim it was built in 1868 and has been restored.

A visit to Eagle Lighthouse and a climb to Eagle Tower will enhance your visit. The park's facilities include a sand bathing beach, numerous picnic areas, a nature center and several hundred campsites. Naturalist programs are conducted from June to September.

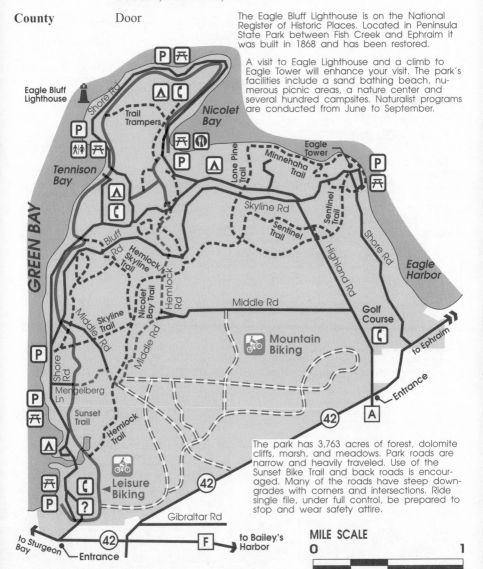

The park has 3,763 acres of forest, dolomite cliffs, marsh, and meadows. Park roads are narrow and heavily traveled. Use of the Sunset Bike Trail and back roads is encouraged. Many of the roads have steep downgrades with corners and intersections. Ride single file, under full control, be prepared to stop and wear safety attire.

MILE SCALE
0   1

Ahnapee State Trail

Trail Length	32 miles (plus another 17 miles planned)
Surface	Limestone screenings
Uses	Bicycling, x-c skiing, snowmobiling, hiking
Location & Setting	The trail is located in east central Wisconsin. The Ahnapee State Trail travels through several legs on abandoned railbed; from Algoma to Sturgeon Bay; from Algoma to Casco Junction; a planned leg from Casco Junction to Brown County and from Luxemburg to Kewaunee. The trails traverse the Ahnapee River. The setting is wooded areas and small communities.
Information	Wisconsin Dept. of Natural Resources 414/492-5821 1125 N. Military Ave. Box 10448 Green Bay, WI 54307-0448 Algoma Area Chamber of Commerce 414/487-2041 Sturgeon Bay Area Information Center 414/743-3924
Counties	Door, Kewaunee

STURGEON BAY
pop. 9176

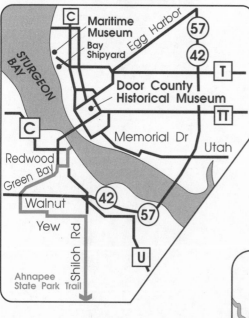

Sturgeon Bay was once a thriving lumber town. Today, ships and luxury yachts are built here for worldwide export. Its historical downtown includes several galleries and museums. Cherry blossom time is in late May and harvest in August draws many to this Cherryland center.

ALGOMA

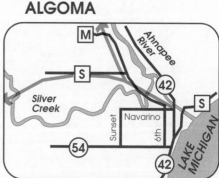

Algoma was originally the site of a Potawatomi Indian Village. Algoma means "Hill of Flowers". The "Campsite" beach area provides almost a mile of lovely sand beach to stroll or to sunbathe. The Von Stiehl Winery in downtown provides guided tours and tasting. There are daily walking tours of historic Algoma from the visitor's Center, located at 1226 Lake St. and overlooking Lake Michigan.

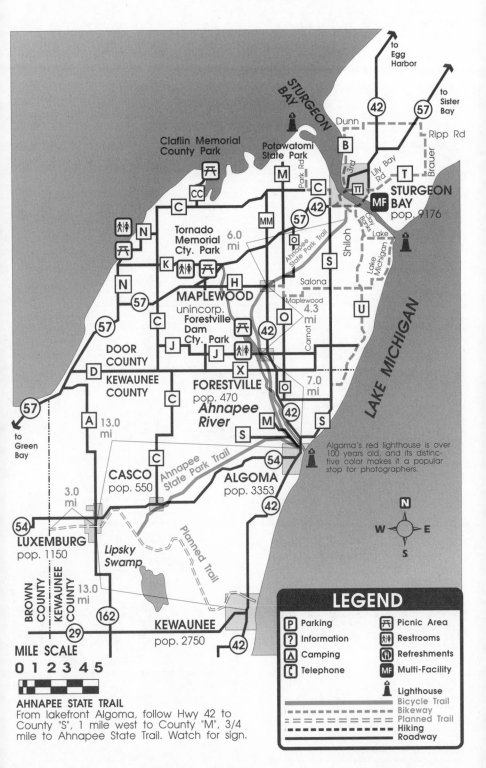

to Egg Harbor

to Sister Bay

STURGEON BAY

Dunn

Ripp Rd

Brauer

Lily Bay Rd

STURGEON BAY
pop. 9176

Claflin Memorial County Park

Potawatomi State Park

Park Rd

Shiloh

Lake

Clay Banks

Lake Michigan

Tornado Memorial Cty. Park

6.0 mi

Ahnapee State Park Trail

Salona

MAPLEWOOD
unincorp.
Forestville Dam Cty. Park

Maplewood
4.3 mi

Carnot

DOOR COUNTY

KEWAUNEE COUNTY

FORESTVILLE
pop. 470
Ahnapee River

7.0 mi

to Green Bay

LAKE MICHIGAN

Ahnapee State Park Trail

CASCO
pop. 550

ALGOMA
pop. 3353

Algoma's red lighthouse is over 100 years old, and its distinctive color makes it a popular stop for photographers.

N
W E
S

3.0 mi

LUXEMBURG
pop. 1150

Lipsky Swamp

Planned Trail

BROWN COUNTY
KEWAUNEE COUNTY

13.0 mi

KEWAUNEE
pop. 2750

MILE SCALE

0 1 2 3 4 5

AHNAPEE STATE TRAIL
From lakefront Algoma, follow Hwy 42 to County "S", 1 mile west to County "M", 3/4 mile to Ahnapee State Trail. Watch for sign.

LEGEND

P	Parking	🥾	Picnic Area
?	Information	🚻	Restrooms
A	Camping	🍴	Refreshments
☎	Telephone	MF	Multi-Facility

⚓ Lighthouse

Bicycle Trail
Bikeway
Planned Trail
Hiking
Roadway

Old Plank Road Trail

Trail Length	17 miles
Surface	Asphalt - 8' wide, with a parallel 8' turf surface
Uses	Bicycling, in-line skating, x-c skiing, snowmobiling, hiking, horseback riding
Location & Setting	The Old Plank Road Trail is in east central Wisconsin. The trail parallels Hwy. 23 from Sheboygan to Greenbush. The setting is farmland, open areas, and small towns.
Information	Sheboygan County Planning & Resources Dept. 414/459-3060 Courthouse, Sheboygan, WI, 53081
County	Sheboygan

Greenbush is the western trailhead and entrance to the Kettle Moraine State Park.

Plan to visit The Old Wade House, a 19th century stagecoach inn, off Hwy. 23.

MILEAGE
Sheboygan Trailhead to Meadowlark Road Trailhead - 4 miles
Meadowlark Road Trailhead to Plymouth Trailhead - 5 miles
Plymouth Trailhead to Greenbush Trailhead - 8 miles
Total - 17 miles

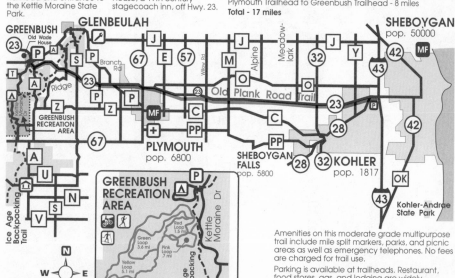

Amenities on this moderate grade multipurpose trail include mile split markers, parks, and picnic areas as well as emergency telephones. No fees are charged for trail use.

Parking is available at trailheads. Restaurant, food stores, gas, and lodging are widely available in communities along the trail corridor.

EAST TRAILHEAD

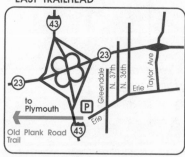

The east trailhead is at the intersection of Hwy. 43 and Hwy. 23. Exit 43 onto 23 and proceed east 1 mile to Taylor Avenue. Turn right on Taylor to Erie Street. Turn right on Erie to the end of the road which is the trailhead. The trail passes under Hwy. 43.

LEGEND

P	Parking	🖼	Picnic Area
🚻	Restroom	🛏	Lodging
?	Information	🍴	Refreshments
🏠	Shelter	🔧	Bicycle Service
MF	Multi-Facility	✚	First Aid

━━━ Bicycle Trail
━━━ Mtn. Biking Trail
- - - - Hiking Trail
━━━ Roadway

Hartman Creek State Park

Trail Length	5.5 miles open to biking (14 miles total)
Surface	Limestone screenings
Uses	Bicycling, x-c skiing, hiking
Location & Setting	The Park is located on the upper Waupaca Chain O'Lakes in central Wisconsin. From Waupaca take Hwy. 49, then Hwy. 54 west about 4 miles to Hartman Creek Road. South 2 miles to the Park entrance. The setting is lakes, open areas, and woods.
Information	Hartman Creek State Park 715/258-2372 N2480 Hartman Creek Road Waupaca, WI 54981-9727
Counties	Waupaca, Portage

The park's facilities include camping, swimming, picnicking, shelters, boating, and fishing. There is a boat launch at the end of Knight Lake Road south of Golke Road.

Trails designated for off-road bicycling are marked with signs. Bicycling is permitted only on those trails signed open and on the roads throughout the park.

AREA OVERVIEW

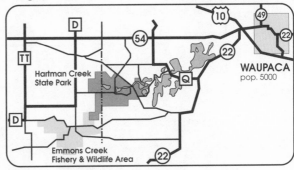

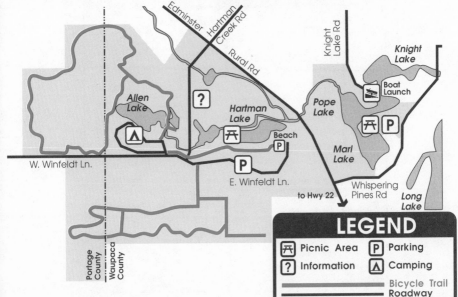

Wiowash Trail
Oshkosh Trails & Bikeways

Trail Length	20 miles
Surface	Limestone screenings
Uses	Bicycling, horseback riding, snowmobiling, hiking
Location & Setting	The Wiowish Trail was built on an abandoned railroad bed and runs from the northwest outskirts of Oshkosh to Hortonville in east central Wisconsin. The setting is open country, farmland, and small communities.

Information	Winnebago County Dept. of Parks 500 East County Road Y, Oshkosh, WI 54901	414/424-0042
	Outagamie County Parks Route #, Plamann Park, Appleton, WI 54915	414/733-3019
Counties	Winnebago, Outagamie	

OSHKOSH TRAILS & BIKEWAYS

POINTS OF INTEREST

Ⓐ Buckstaff Observatory
Ⓑ Paine Art Center and Arboretum
Ⓒ Wittman Airport and Experimental Aircraft Museum
Ⓓ Menominee Park
Ⓔ University of Wisconsin-Oshkosh
Ⓕ Winnebago County Park

HORTONVILLE
pop. 2000

Food and lodging available in Hortonville. Picnic area at Hwy. 45 exit.

NORTH TRAILHEAD

Trail Access: Exit Hwy. 45 onto Hwy. M (Nash Street) for 2 blocks to Lake Shore Drive. Follow this road around the lake for about a mile. There is parking but no designated facilities.

WIOWASH TRAIL ROUTE SLIP:

Oshkosh (HWY 41)	SEGMENT	TOTAL
HWY GG	3.5	3.5
HWY 150	6.5	10.0
HWY 10	5.5	15.5
Hortonville	4.5	20.0

Spring Rd   4.5 mi

School Rd

MEDINA

Hunters

5.5 mi

Rat River Bridge

USE CAUTION WHEN CROSSING RR TRACKS

Medina Junction Rd

N. Loop Rd.

MEDINA JUNCTION

Winnegamie

Outagamie County

Winnebago County

APPLETON
pop. 65700

College

LARSEN

BUSY HWY. CROSSING

Oakridge Rd

NEENAH

Lakeview

Breezewood Ln

Indian Shores Rd

6.5 mi

Maxwell Rd

Daggets Creek

High Trestle Bridge

Brooks Rd

Sunnyview

Ryf

3.5 mi

BUSY HWY. CROSSING
Westwind Rd

LAKE BUTTE DES MORTS

LAKE WINNEBAGO

N
W   E
S

LEGEND

🏞 Picnic Area		P Parking	
? Information		🚻 Restrooms	
⛲ Drinking Fountain		🏪 Refreshments	
🛏 Lodging		🔧 Bicycle Service	
MF Multi-Facility			
⚓ Lighthouse			

- - - - - Bicycle Trail
- - - - - Bikeway
——— Roadway

OSHKOSH
pop. 55000

SOUTH TRAILHEAD

Trail can be accessed from West Wind Road just southwest of the intersection of HWY 41 and HWY 110, there is parking at the intersection of HWY 110 and CTH Y (Sunnyview Rd.).

MILE SCALE
0   1   2   3   4   5

Mountain-Bay Trail

Trail Length	83.4 miles
Surface	Compacted granite
Uses	Bicycling, hiking, x-c skiing, snowmobiling, horseback riding, (Shawano County).
Location & Setting	The Mountain-Bay Trail is built on the former Chicago and Northwestern railroad right-of-way in East Central Wisconsin. It stretches over 83 miles from Brown County just west of Green Bay, through Shawano County and into Marathon County to Wausau. Named for the two geological features it connects, Rib Mountain in Marathon County and Green Bay in Brown County.
Information	Brown County Parks 414/448-4466 Box 1600, Green Bay, WI 54305
	Shawano County Parks 715/524-5165 311 N. Main St., Shawano, WI 54166
	Marathon County Parks 715/847-5235 500 Forest St., Wausau, WI 54403
Counties	Brown, Shawano, Marathon

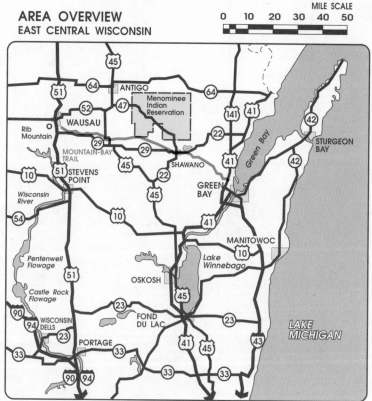

AREA OVERVIEW
EAST CENTRAL WISCONSIN

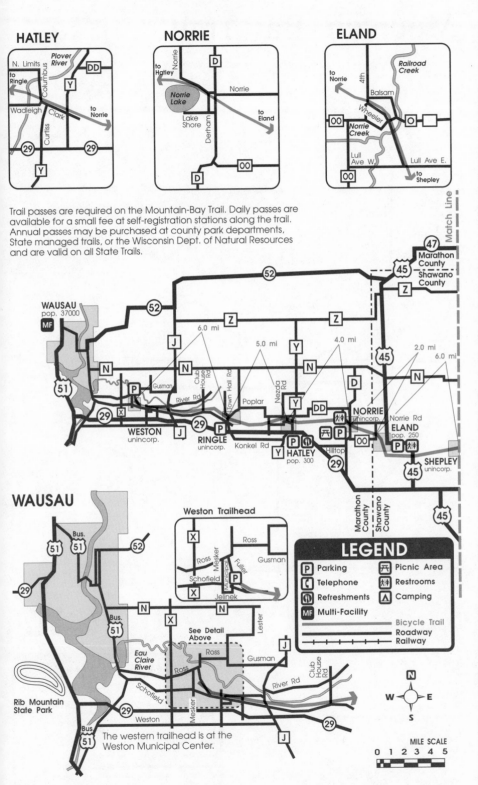

Trail passes are required on the Mountain-Bay Trail. Daily passes are available for a small fee at self-registration stations along the trail. Annual passes may be purchased at county park departments, State managed trails, or the Wisconsin Dept. of Natural Resources and are valid on all State Trails.

Mountain-Bay Trail

Mountain-Bay Trail

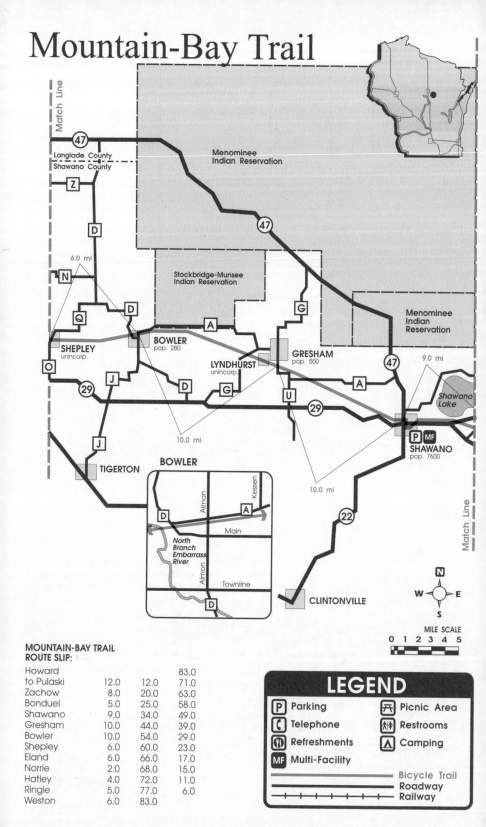

Match Line

47

Langlade County
Shawano County

Menominee
Indian Reservation

Z

D

6.0 mi

47

N

Stockbridge-Munsee
Indian Reservation

Q

D

A

G

Menominee
Indian
Reservation

SHEPLEY
unincorp.

BOWLER
pop. 280

LYNDHURST
unincorp.

GRESHAM
pop. 500

9.0 mi

O

J

D

G

47

Shawano Lake

29

U

A

10.0 mi

29

J

10.0 mi

P **MF**
SHAWANO
pop. 7600

TIGERTON

BOWLER

Almon

Kessen

D

A

Main

North
Branch
Embarrass
River

22

Almon

Townline

D

CLINTONVILLE

N
W—E
S

**MOUNTAIN-BAY TRAIL
ROUTE SLIP:**

Howard			83.0
to Pulaski	12.0	12.0	71.0
Zachow	8.0	20.0	63.0
Bonduel	5.0	25.0	58.0
Shawano	9.0	34.0	49.0
Gresham	10.0	44.0	39.0
Bowler	10.0	54.0	29.0
Shepley	6.0	60.0	23.0
Eland	6.0	66.0	17.0
Norrie	2.0	68.0	15.0
Hatley	4.0	72.0	11.0
Ringle	5.0	77.0	6.0
Weston	6.0	83.0	

LEGEND

P	Parking	**⚏**	Picnic Area
C	Telephone	**⚏**	Restrooms
⚏	Refreshments	**A**	Camping
MF	Multi-Facility		

Bicycle Trail
Roadway
Railway

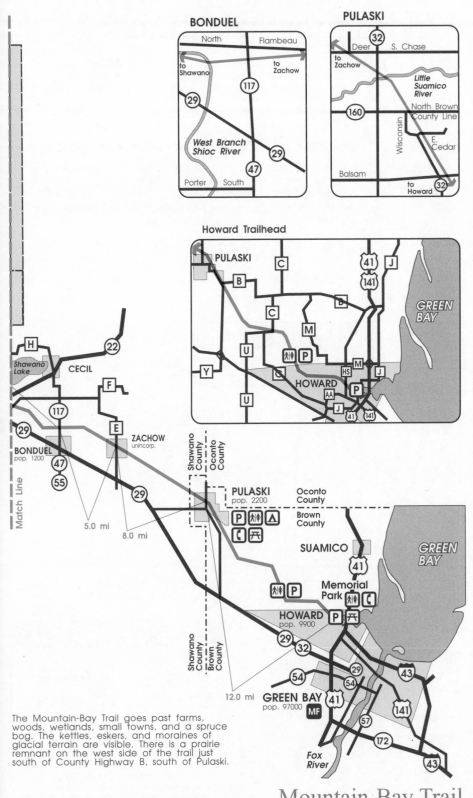

BONDUEL

North
Flambeau
to Shawano
to Zachow
117
29
West Branch Shioc River
47
Porter
South

PULASKI

32
Deer
S. Chase
to Zachow
Little Suamico River
160
North Brown County Line
Wisconsin
E. Cedar
Balsam
to Howard
32

Howard Trailhead

PULASKI
C
B
41
141
J
C
D
M
U
GREEN BAY
Y
C
M
HS
J
HOWARD
AA
P
U
J
41
141

22
H
Shawano Lake
CECIL
F
117
E
ZACHOW
unincorp.
29
BONDUEL
pop. 1200
47
55
29
Shawano County
Oconto County
PULASKI
pop. 2200
Oconto County
Brown County
5.0 mi
8.0 mi
P
SUAMICO
GREEN BAY
41
Memorial Park
Shawano County
Brown County
HOWARD
pop. 9900
P
29
32
29
54
43
12.0 mi
54
GREEN BAY
pop. 97000
MF
41
141
57
172
Fox River
43

Match Line

The Mountain-Bay Trail goes past farms, woods, wetlands, small towns, and a spruce bog. The kettles, eskers, and moraines of glacial terrain are visible. There is a prairie remnant on the west side of the trail just south of County Highway B, south of Pulaski.

Mountain-Bay Trail

Wild Goose State Trail

Trail Length	34.5 miles
Surface	Limestone screenings
Uses	Bicycling, x-c skiing, hiking, snowmobiling, horseback riding
Location & Setting	Located in southeast Wisconsin, following an abandoned railbed between Fond du Lac and Clyman. The trail parallels the western side on the Horicon Marsh Wildlife Area and National Wildlife Refuge. The route is tree lined with wildflowers, woodlots, wildlife, farm fields, prairie remnants, and glacial end moraines.
Information	Friends of the Recreation Trail (F.O.R.T.) 414/485-2917 P.O. Box 72, Juneau, WI 53039
Counties	Dodge, Fond du Lac

FOND DU LAC

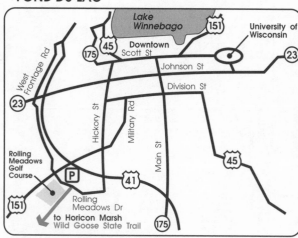

FOND DU LAC
Bordered on the north by Lake Winnebago, the largest freshwater lake in Wisconsin. Points of interest include the "Talking Houses and Historic Places" tour and historic Galloway House and Village.

PARKING IN FOND DU LAC
Suggestions: Rolling Meadows Golf Course, just west of the north trailhead, Marsh Haven Nature Center and the Horicon National Wildlife Refuge just east of the trail at Hwy 49, the Juneau City Park on Lincoln Street, and at the intersections of Hwy 33 and 26.

HORICON MARSH is an extinct glacial lake and the largest freshwater cattail marsh in the United States. It's known as the "Little Everglades of the North." The marsh supports diverse wildlife and plants, including threatened species such as great egrets, bald eagles, osprey, and peregrine falcons. Horicon Marsh is a major migration stopover for the Mississippi valley population of Canada geese during their travels between Hudson Bay and southern Illinois/western Kentucky. Over 100,000 descend on Horicon Marsh in spring and fall.

LEGEND

🎑	Picnic Area	P	Parking
?	Information	🚹	Restrooms
🍴	Refreshments	C	Telephone
🛏	Lodging	▲	Camping
MF	Multi-Facility		

━━━━━━━ Bicycle Trail
========= Planned Trail
▪▪▪▪▪▪▪▪▪ Bikeway
━━━━━━━ Roadway

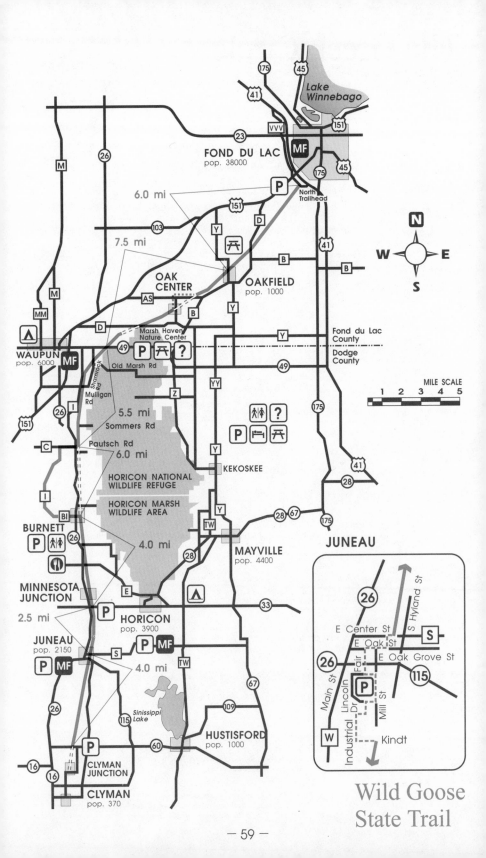

Wild Goose
State Trail

The Green Circle

Trail Length	22 miles
Surface	Asphalt, crushed granite, wood chips
Uses	Bicycling, x-c skiing, hiking/jogging
Location & Setting	The Green Circle is located in Stevens Point Wisconsin. Much of the trail system parallels the Wisconsin and Plover Rivers as they flow through the city and then join. The setting is greenways (parks) and urban.
Information	Green Circle Committee 715/344-1941 2442 Sims Ave., Stevens Point, WI 54481 Stevens Point Parks & Recreation 715/346-1536
County	Portage

A. Riverfront Trail
Trail starts near Bank One where Hwy. 10 crosses the Wisconsin River. Goes North about 1.3 miles through Bukolt Park. Park at Bukolt or near the Bank One/Chamber lots. (**Hike, Bike**)

B. Stagecoach Trail

C. Holiday Trail
Start at either the SE corner of the Zenoff Softball Park or off Northpoint Drive about one block West of the Holiday Inn. Okay to park on Northpoint Drive. This trail is crushed red granite about .9 mile. (**Hike, Bike**)

D. University Trail
Can be accessed in three spots: **1-**On the south side of North Point Drive, across from Sentry Insurance. **2-**At the northeast corner of Michigan Ave. and Maria Drive. **3-**At Schmeeckle Reserve Visitor Center on Northpoint Drive about a block east of Michigan Ave. Trail loops University Lake. (**Hike**)

E. Moses Creek Trail

F. Plover River Trail
Access in two spots: **1-**At the east end of Barbara's Lane. (Go east on Hwy. 10 to Green Ave. in Park Ridge. Turn north to Jordan Lane then east on Janick Circle which becomes Barbara's Lane). **2-**east on Hwy. 66 past the airport and Torun Rd. to the Ski Lodge just past the Izaak Walton entrance on the south side of Hwy. 66. Trail goes 6.2 miles. (**Hike, Bike, Ski**)

G. Iverson Park Trail
This 1.3 mile trail loops from the parking lot in Iverson Park at the foot of Hillcrest Drive (Jefferson Street). Go to Park Ridge on Hwy. 10 East, turn south on Sunrise Ave. to Hillcrest Dr. Turn east through the gateway downhill to the parking lot. (**Hike, Bike, Ski**)

H. McDill Trail
Start either at Hwy. HH one block east of Feltz Ave. or at Heffron St. between Feltz Ave. and Leahy Ave. or on Patch St. just east of the bridge. This trail extends about two miles from Patch St. to Hwy HH. (**Hike,Bike**)

I. Whiting Park Trail
Access in two spots: **1-**near the traffic light corner of McDill Road (Hwy HH) and Post Rd. (Business 51). **2-**Turn west off Post Road on Cedar St. to the dead end. Trail extends about one mile along the Plover River. (**Hike**)

J. Paper Mills Trail

K. River Pines Trail
Starts from the western parking lot of Stevens Point Nursing/Rehab Center (which is at the western end of Sherman Ave.) Parallels the river about 1.6 miles to the City Wastewater Plant at the west end of Bliss Ave. (Parking). It continues up to Bliss Ave. to Tamarack to Wisconsin to Water St. to Bank One where the Riverfront Trail begins. (**Hike, Bike**)

L. Hoover Road Trail
Drive on Hwy. 10 East to the Budgetel Motel. Turn south at the traffic light on Country Club Drive (which becomes Hoover Road). Proceed about one mile to Ponderosa St. where the trail begins. It continues south to Lake Pacawa for more than 2 miles (**Hike, Bike**)

Stevens Point - pop. 23000

Wisconsin River

B Stagecoach Trail

A Riverfront Trail

N. Second St

Bukolt

Michigan Ave

C Holiday Trail

Northpoint Dr

Bus. 51

D University Trail

University Lake

66

Centerpoint Dr

Main St

Clark St

Jefferson St

Wisconsin River

Bliss

Patch St

Water St

Bus. 51

K River Pines Trail

Sherman Ave

W. River Rd

J Paper Mills Trail

Cedar St

Michigan Ave

G Iverson Trail

H McDill Trail

Feltz

McDill Pond

I Whiting Park Trail

Porter Rd

E Moses Creek Trail

66

F Plover River Trail

Stevens Point Municipal Airport

Sunset

Greenbriar

51

Plover River

Park Ridge Dr.

10

Plover River

Country Club Drive

HH

HH

51

Little Plover River

P

L Hoover Road Trail

Hoover Rd

Post Rd

Bus. 51

54

Plover Rd

LEGEND

🏕 Picnic Area   **P** Parking

? Information   **A** Camping

━━ Bicycle Trail
━━ Roadway

The Green Circle

CE Trail

Trail Length	4.2 miles
Surface	Asphalt
Uses	Bicycling, in-line skating, x-c skiing, hiking/jogging
Location & Setting	The CE Trail is a corridor linking the Outagamie County cities of Appleton and Kaukauna. The trail parallels the north side of County Highway CE between Hwy. 441 in Appleton and Hwy. 55 in Kaukauna
Information	Outagamie County 414/832-5255 401 Walnut Street, Appleton, WI 54911-5936
County	Outagamie

AREA OVERVIEW - Appleton to Kaukauna

Bicycle Trail
Planned Trails
& Bikewaysl

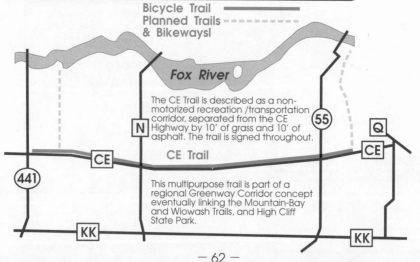

Fox River

The CE Trail is described as a non-motorized recreation /transportation corridor, separated from the CE Highway by 10' of grass and 10' of asphalt. The trail is signed throughout.

CE Trail

This multipurpose trail is part of a regional Greenway Corridor concept eventually linking the Mountain-Bay and Wiowash Trails, and High Cliff State Park.

Omaha Trail

Trail Length	12.5 miles
Surface	Paved
Uses	Bicycling, hiking, in-line skating
Location & Setting	The Omaha Trail runs from Elroy to Camp Douglas just south of Interstate I90/94. The trail includes 17 bridges, an overpass, and a 850 foot long tunnel.
Information	Land, Forestry, and Parks Dept. 250 Oak Street, Mauston, WI 53948 608/847-9389
County	Juneau

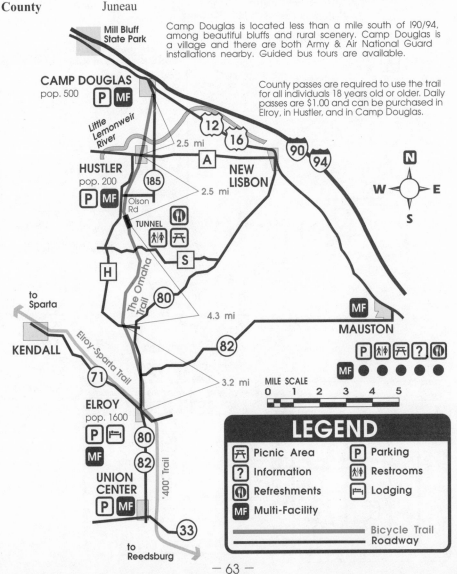

Camp Douglas is located less than a mile south of I90/94, among beautiful bluffs and rural scenery. Camp Douglas is a village and there are both Army & Air National Guard installations nearby. Guided bus tours are available.

County passes are required to use the trail for all individuals 18 years old or older. Daily passes are $1.00 and can be purchased in Elroy, in Hustler, and in Camp Douglas.

LEGEND

- Picnic Area
- Information
- Refreshments
- MF Multi-Facility
- P Parking
- Restrooms
- Lodging
- Bicycle Trail
- Roadway

Elroy-Sparta State Trail

Trail Length	32 miles
Surface	Limestone screenings
Uses	Bicycling, x-c skiing, snowmobiling, hiking
Location & Setting	The Elroy-Sparta State trail is located in west central Wisconsin and runs between the communities of Elroy and Sparta on abandoned railbed. The entire corridor is a wildlife refuge.
Information	Sparta Area Chamber of Commerce 608/269-4123 111 Milwaukee Street, Sparta, WI 54656-2576 Elroy-Sparta National Trail 608/463-7109 P.O. Box 297, Kendall, WI 54638
Counties	Monroe, Juneau

SPARTA
pop. 7788

Facilities available at the Sparta depot include parking, restrooms, water, information and telephone.

ROUTE SLIP	INTERVAL	TOTAL
Elroy (Trailhead)		
33rd	3.5	3.5
Kendall	2.5	6.0
Tunnel #1 (.25m)	3.0*	9.0
27th St.	2.5	11.5
Wilton	3.5	15.0
Tunnel #2 (.25m)	2.0*	17.0
Norwalk	4.0	21.0
Tunnel #3 (.75m)	3.0*	24.0
Dalton Ave.	5.2	29.2
Sparta (Trailhead)	2.8	32.0
*To tunnel mid-point		

SPARTA, known as the "Bicycling Capital of America", is the connecting point to the northern end of the Elroy-Sparta Bike Trail and the eastern end of the LaCrosse River Bike Trail.

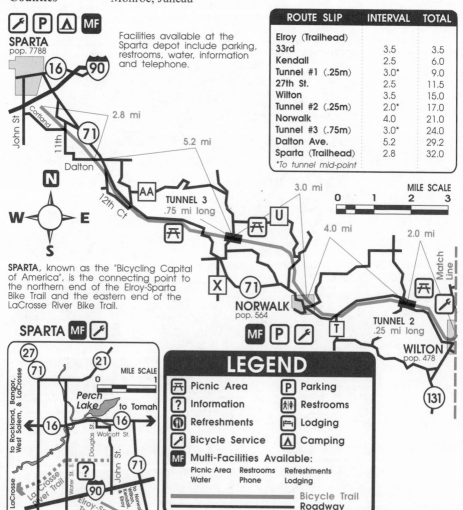

LEGEND

- 🎋 Picnic Area
- ? Information
- 🏪 Refreshments
- 🔧 Bicycle Service
- **MF** Multi-Facilities Available:
- P Parking
- 🚻 Restrooms
- 🛏 Lodging
- ⛺ Camping

Picnic Area   Restrooms   Refreshments
Water   Phone   Lodging

▬▬▬ Bicycle Trail
——— Roadway

AREA OVERVIEW

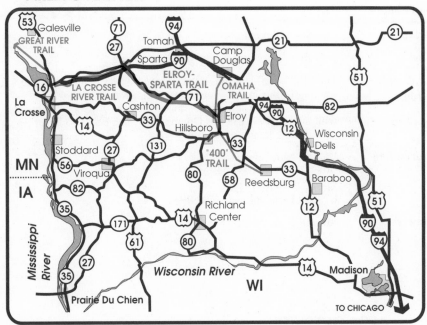

The Elroy-Sparta State Trail was established in 1965. The trail is noted for its three tunnels; the longest, Tunnel Three, is three-quarter miles. Bikes must be walked through the tunnels which are cool and dark, so bring along a flashlight and a wrap.

DRIVER SERVICE
Located in Kendall at Trail Headquarters. A driver will take your vehicle to take you where you wish to begin your bike trip. Your vehicle will be waiting at your destination. There is a nominal fee. Call (608) 463-7109 for reservations.

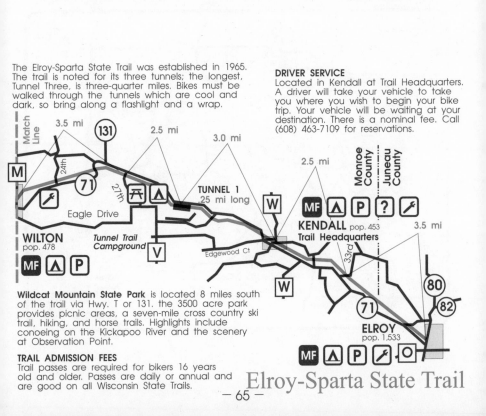

Wildcat Mountain State Park is located 8 miles south of the trail via Hwy. T or 131. the 3500 acre park provides picnic areas, a seven-mile cross country ski trail, hiking, and horse trails. Highlights include conoeing on the Kickapoo River and the scenery at Observation Point.

TRAIL ADMISSION FEES
Trail passes are required for bikers 16 years old and older. Passes are daily or annual and are good on all Wisconsin State Trails.

Elroy-Sparta State Trail

"400" Trail

Trail Length	27.5 miles
Surface	Limestone screenings
Uses	Bicycling, x-c skiing, snowmobiling, hiking
Location & Setting	The "400" Trail is a converted Chicago-Northwestern rail line running from Elroy to Reedsburg. This 28 mile trail, which includes a 5-mile spur from Union Center to Hillsboro, connects with the Elroy-Sparta and Omaha Trail. The Baraboo River parallels the length of the trail.
Information	Wildcat Mountain State Park 608/337-4775 Box 99, Ontario, WI 54651
	Mirror Lake State Park 608/254-2333 E10320 Fern Dell Rd., WI 53913
Counties	Juneau, Sauk, Vernon

AREA OVERVIEW

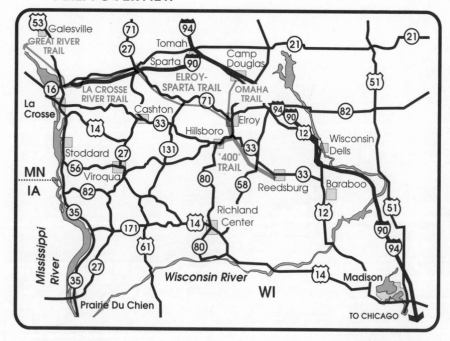

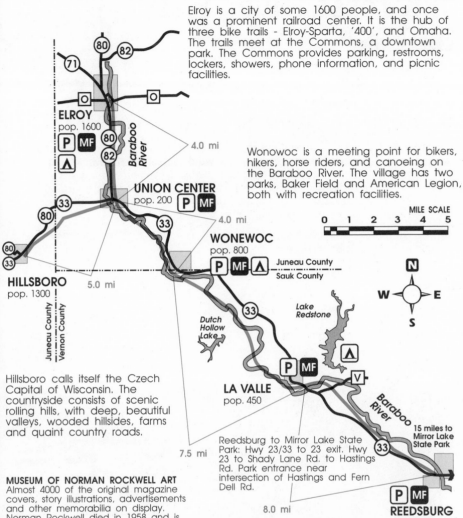

Elroy is a city of some 1600 people, and once was a prominent railroad center. It is the hub of three bike trails - Elroy-Sparta, '400', and Omaha. The trails meet at the Commons, a downtown park. The Commons provides parking, restrooms, lockers, showers, phone information, and picnic facilities.

Wonowoc is a meeting point for bikers, hikers, horse riders, and canoeing on the Baraboo River. The village has two parks, Baker Field and American Legion, both with recreation facilities.

Hillsboro calls itself the Czech Capital of Wisconsin. The countryside consists of scenic rolling hills, with deep, beautiful valleys, wooded hillsides, farms and quaint country roads.

Reedsburg to Mirror Lake State Park: Hwy 23/33 to 23 exit. Hwy 23 to Shady Lane Rd. to Hastings Rd. Park entrance near intersection of Hastings and Fern Dell Rd.

MUSEUM OF NORMAN ROCKWELL ART
Almost 4000 of the original magazine covers, story illustrations, advertisements and other memorabilia on display. Norman Rockwell died in 1958 and is known as the "artist of the people." Open daily - year round. 227 S. Park St., Reedsburg; 608/524-2123

MID-CONTINENT RAILWAY
Experience a Steam Train ride from the early 1900s. Four trips daily from mid-May to Labor Day and on weekends til mid-October. North Freedom, WI 53951; 608/522-4261

PIONEER LOG VILLAGE AND MUSEUM
Log library, log church, 3 log houses, blacksmith shop, country school, country store and 3 museum buildings. Hwy 23 & 33, 3 miles east of Reedsburg. Open weekends from Memorial weekend through September. Donations only.

MODEL RAILROAD MUSEUM
Operating Layouts. Thousands of models on display. Near the Wisconsin Dells. For directions call 608/254-8050.

Reedsburg is a city of 5000. It is within 30 miles of Wisconsin Dells, Circus World Museum, Devils Lake State Park, a Railway Museum and the House on the Rock. Its own attractions include the Pioneer Village and Museum of Norman Rockwell Art. There are two antique malls with over 40 dealers.

LEGEND

🖼 Picnic Area	Ⓟ Parking
? Information	🚹 Restrooms
Ⓜ Refreshments	🛏 Lodging
MF Multi-Facility	⛺ Camping
▬▬▬ Bicycle Trail	
▬▬▬ Roadway	

LaCrosse River Trail

Trail Length	21.5 miles
Surface	Limestone screenings
Uses	Bicycling, hiking, x-c skiing, snowmobiling
Location & Setting	The trail parallels the LaCrosse River and is a connecting link between the Elroy-Sparta and the Great River trails. It was developed from the abandoned Chicago and Northwestern Railroad between Sparta and Medary Junction, just outside of LaCrosse. Farmlands, wooded hillsides, trout streams and Neshonoc Lake adorn the trail.
Information	Wildcat Mountain State Park 608/337-4775 Box 99, Ontario, WI 54651
Counties	Monroe, LaCrosse

La Crosse sits on the convergence of three rivers, the LaCrosse River, the Black River, and the Mississippi River. The area was first visited by Father Louis Hennepin in 1680. Permanent settlement began in 1841.

Match Line

Great River Trail

LAKE ONALASKA

Upper Mississippi River National Wildlife and Fish Refuge

53

35   Onalaska Park   P

ONALASKA pop. 11300

157

OS

LaCrosse Municipal Airport

90

La Crosse River

Veterans Memorial Park

90

108

P   WEST SALEM pop.3600

16

Lake Neshonoc

M

B

7.0 mi

B

P   ?

MEDARY unincorp.

53

35

16

LA CROSSE pop. 51000

P

?   Bicycle Service

14   61

16

16

26   Minnesota

14   Wisconsin

61

35

14   61

Upper Mississippi River National Wildlife and Fish Refuge

MEDARY

35   Center for Commerce & Tourism   45   Oak Forest Drive

157   Onalaska Park   P   90

?

Ash

LaCrosse Municipal Airport

16

Bridge

LaCrosse River   16

90   35

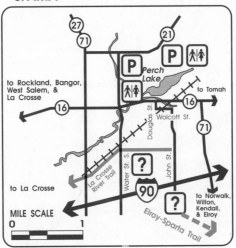

SPARTA

to Rockland, Bangor, West Salem, & La Crosse

Perch Lake

to Tomah

Wolcott St.

Douglas St.

Water St. S.

John St.

to La Crosse

to Norwalk, Wilton, Kendall, & Elroy

La Crosse River Trail

Elroy-Sparta Trail

MILE SCALE
0   1

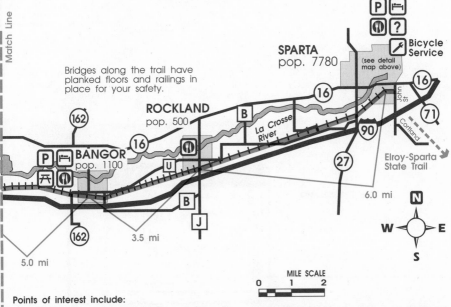

Match Line

Bridges along the trail have planked floors and railings in place for your safety.

SPARTA pop. 7780

Bicycle Service

(see detail map above)

ROCKLAND pop. 500

La Crosse River

BANGOR pop. 1100

Elroy-Sparta State Trail

6.0 mi

3.5 mi

5.0 mi

N
W   E
S

MILE SCALE
0   1   2

Points of interest include:

Grandad Bluff - a 600 foot bluff overlooking the city of LaCrosse and the Mississippi River Valley. It affords a view of three states.

Excursion Boats - there are several river excursion boats based in LaCrosse.

G. Heileman Brewery - offers tours and an opportunity to sample their products.

TRAIL ADMISSION FEES

Trail passes are required for bikers 16 years old and older. Fees varies as to whether resident or non-resident, and whether daily or seasonal. Passes are good on all Wisconsin State trails.

LEGEND

🎪 Picnic Area	P Parking
? Information	🚻 Restrooms
🔧 Bicycle Service	⛺ Camping
➕ First Aid	🛏 Lodging
MF Multi-Facility	🍴 Refreshments

▬▬▬ Bicycle Trail
━━━ Roadway
━┼━┼━ Railway

La Crosse River Trail

Great River State Trail

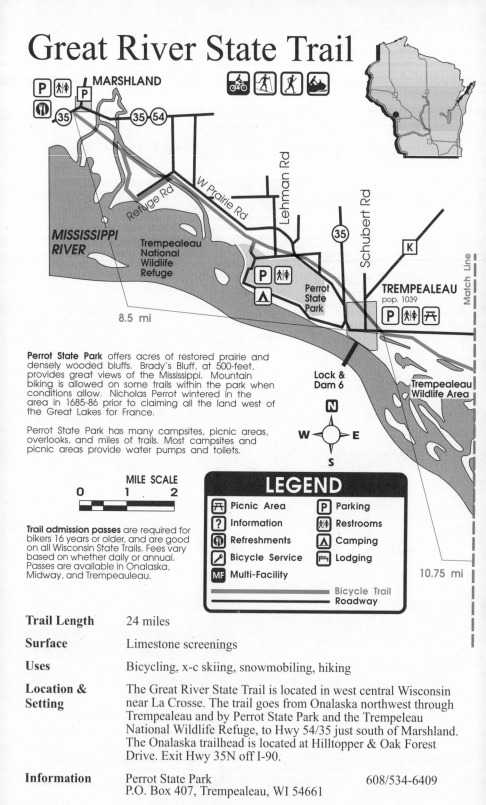

MARSHLAND

MISSISSIPPI RIVER

Trempealeau National Wildlife Refuge

8.5 mi

W Prairie Rd

Refuge Rd

Lehman Rd

Schubert Rd

Perrot State Park

Lock & Dam 6

TREMPEALEAU
pop. 1039

Trempealeau Wildlife Area

Match Line

K

35 35-54 35

N
W E
S

10.75 mi

Perrot State Park offers acres of restored prairie and densely wooded bluffs. Brady's Bluff, at 500-feet, provides great views of the Mississippi. Mountain biking is allowed on some trails within the park when conditions allow. Nicholas Perrot wintered in the area in 1685-86 prior to claiming all the land west of the Great Lakes for France.

Perrot State Park has many campsites, picnic areas, overlooks, and miles of trails. Most campsites and picnic areas provide water pumps and toilets.

MILE SCALE
0   1   2

Trail admission passes are required for bikers 16 years or older, and are good on all Wisconsin State Trails. Fees vary based on whether daily or annual. Passes are available in Onalaska, Midway, and Trempeauleau.

LEGEND

🏕 Picnic Area		P Parking	
? Information		🚻 Restrooms	
🛒 Refreshments		⛺ Camping	
🔧 Bicycle Service		🏠 Lodging	
MF Multi-Facility			

━━━ Bicycle Trail
━━━ Roadway

Trail Length	24 miles
Surface	Limestone screenings
Uses	Bicycling, x-c skiing, snowmobiling, hiking
Location & Setting	The Great River State Trail is located in west central Wisconsin near La Crosse. The trail goes from Onalaska northwest through Trempealeau and by Perrot State Park and the Trempeleau National Wildlife Refuge, to Hwy 54/35 just south of Marshland. The Onalaska trailhead is located at Hilltopper & Oak Forest Drive. Exit Hwy 35N off I-90.
Information	Perrot State Park 608/534-6409
	P.O. Box 407, Trempealeau, WI 54661
Counties	La Crosse, Trempealeau

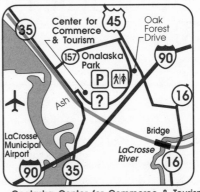

ONALASKA

Center for Commerce & Tourism

Oak Forest Drive

Onalaska Park

LaCrosse Municipal Airport

Ash

Bridge

LaCrosse River

Onalaska Center for Commerce & Tourism
800 Oak Forest Drive
Onalaska, WI 54650

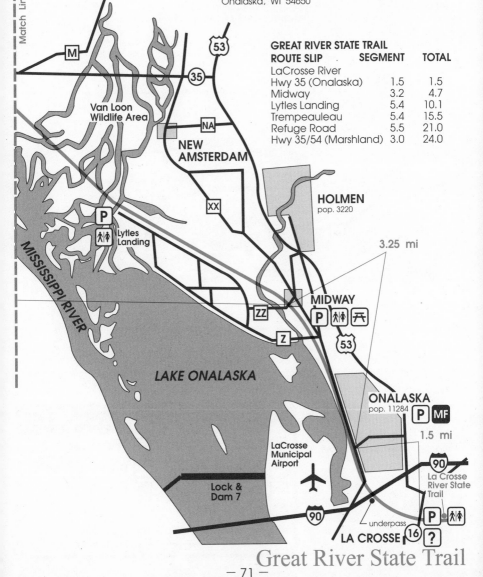

Match Line

Van Loon Wildlife Area

NEW AMSTERDAM

HOLMEN
pop. 3220

Lytles Landing

MISSISSIPPI RIVER

LAKE ONALASKA

MIDWAY

3.25 mi

ONALASKA
pop. 11284

1.5 mi

La Crosse River State Trail

LaCrosse Municipal Airport

Lock & Dam 7

underpass

LA CROSSE

GREAT RIVER STATE TRAIL

ROUTE SLIP	SEGMENT	TOTAL
LaCrosse River		
Hwy 35 (Onalaska)	1.5	1.5
Midway	3.2	4.7
Lytles Landing	5.4	10.1
Trempeauleau	5.4	15.5
Refuge Road	5.5	21.0
Hwy 35/54 (Marshland)	3.0	24.0

Great River State Trail

Red Cedar State Park Trail

Trail Length	14.5 miles
Surface	Limestone screenings
Uses	Bicycling, x-c skiing, hiking
Location & Setting	The Red Cedar Trail is located in west central Wisconsin. The trail is built on abandoned railbed paralleling the Red Cedar River between Menomonie and Chippewa River southeast of Dunnville. Beautiful bluffs and views of the river accompany much of the route.
Information	Trail Coordinator, Wisconsin DNR 715/839-1607 1300 W. Clairemont, Eau Claire, WI 54702
County	Dunn

The Red Cedar Trail is built on a railbed, and includes numerous rock formations and an 800 foot railroad trestle which crosses the Chippewa River. There is a fee for biking or X-C skiing.

AREA OVERVIEW

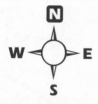

LEGEND

P	Parking	**入人**	Restrooms
架	Picnic Area	**豐**	Drinking Fountain
⌂	Lodging	**⊞**	Refreshments
MF	Multi-Facility		

Bicycle Trail
Roadway

Trail passes are required for bikers 16 years old and older. Passes are daily or annual and are good on all Wisconsin State Trails.

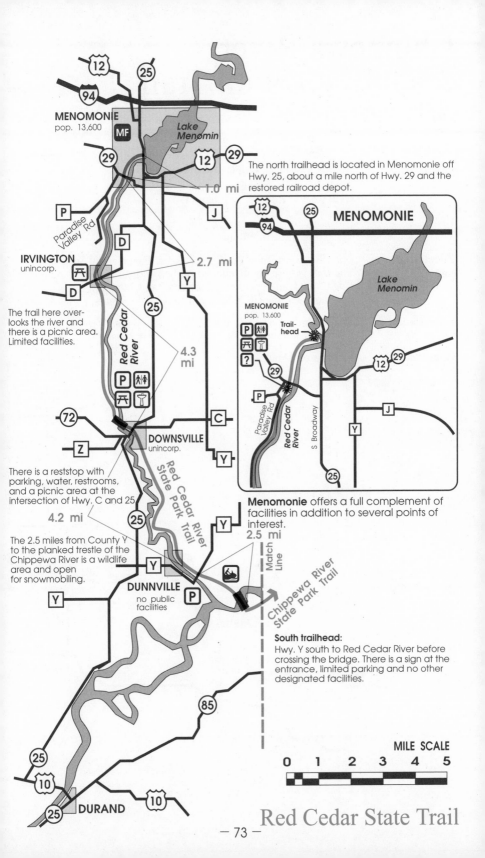

MENOMONIE
pop. 13,600

Lake Menømin

The north trailhead is located in Menomonie off Hwy. 25, about a mile north of Hwy. 29 and the restored railroad depot.

1.0 mi

MENOMONIE

Lake Menomin

MENOMONIE
pop. 13,600

Trail-head

Paradise Valley Rd

S Broadway

Red Cedar River

IRVINGTON
unincorp.

The trail here over-looks the river and there is a picnic area. Limited facilities.

2.7 mi

4.3 mi

Red Cedar River

DOWNSVILLE
unincorp.

Red Cedar River State Park Trail

There is a reststop with parking, water, restrooms, and a picnic area at the intersection of Hwy. C and 25.

Menomonie offers a full complement of facilities in addition to several points of interest.

2.5 mi

4.2 mi

The 2.5 miles from County Y to the planked trestle of the Chippewa River is a wildlife area and open for snowmobiling.

DUNNVILLE
no public facilities

Match Line

Chippewa River State Park Trail

South trailhead:
Hwy. Y south to Red Cedar River before crossing the bridge. There is a sign at the entrance, limited parking and no other designated facilities.

MILE SCALE

0 1 2 3 4 5

DURAND

Red Cedar State Trail

Chippewa River State Recreation Trail

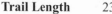

Trail Length	23 miles
Surface	Asphalt (Eau Claire to HWY 85) Asphalt emulsion with pea-stone gravel (HWY 85 to Red Cedar Junciton)
Uses	Bicycling, in-line skating, hiking/jogging, x-c skiing, snowmobiling
Location & Setting	The Chippewa River Trail is located in East Central Wisconsin. The trail is built on abandoned railbed and parallels the south side of the Chippewa River between Eau Claire and the confluence of the Chippewa and Red Cedar Rivers.
Information	Trail Coordinator, Wisconsin DNR 715/839-1607 1300 W. Clairemont, Eau Claire, WI
Counties	Eau Claire, Dunn

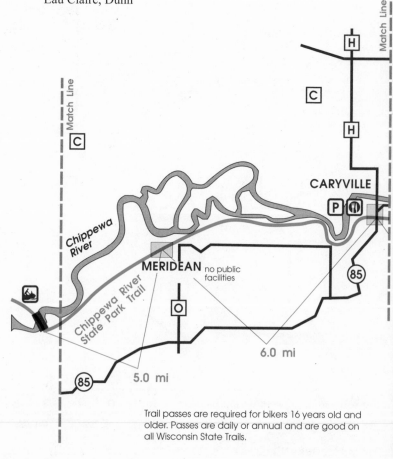

Trail passes are required for bikers 16 years old and
older. Passes are daily or annual and are good on
all Wisconsin State Trails.

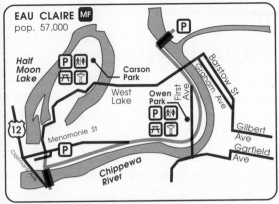

EAU CLAIRE MF
pop. 57,000

Half Moon Lake
Carson Park
West Lake
Owen Park
First Ave
Graham Ave
Barstow St
Gilbert Ave
Garfield Ave
Menomonie St
Clairmont Ave
Chippewa River

Access to water, restrooms, and picnic areas are conveniently located along the Eau Claire trail extension. The city offers a complete selection of facilities and many points of interest.

Bike rentals are available. Other activities include canoeing and pontoon boating, with both rental and tours. Cross country skiing is allowed in the city parks and automobile drag racing off Hwy. 85 in Caryville.

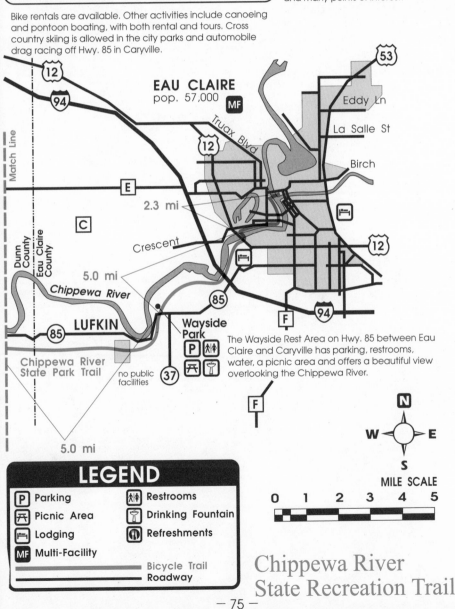

EAU CLAIRE MF
pop. 57,000

Match Line
Truax Blvd
Eddy Ln
La Salle St
Birch
E
2.3 mi
C
Crescent
Dunn County
Eau Claire County
Chippewa River
5.0 mi
LUFKIN
85
Wayside Park
Chippewa River State Park Trail
no public facilities
37
F
5.0 mi

The Wayside Rest Area on Hwy. 85 between Eau Claire and Caryville has parking, restrooms, water, a picnic area and offers a beautiful view overlooking the Chippewa River.

F

N
W   E
S
MILE SCALE
0 1 2 3 4 5

LEGEND

P Parking		👫 Restrooms	
🎪 Picnic Area		🍶 Drinking Fountain	
🛏 Lodging		🍴 Refreshments	
MF Multi-Facility			

Bicycle Trail
Roadway

Chippewa River State Recreation Trail

Buffalo River State Recreation Trail

Trail Length	36.4 miles
Surface	Fine gravel & cinder (eastern portion sandier)
Uses	Bicycling, x-c skiing, snowmobiling, horseback riding, hiking, ATV
Location & Setting	The Buffalo River State Recreation Trail is in West central Wisconsin. The trail is built on converted railbed and follows the Buffalo River between the towns of Mondavi and Fairchild. The setting is open area, farmland, and small communities.
Information	Trail Coordinator, Wisconsin DNR 705/839-1607 1300 W. Clairemont, Eau Claire, WI 54702
Counties	Buffalo, Trempealeau, Jackson

Access the West Trailhead by exiting south onto Marten Rd at the intersection of Hwy. 37 and Hwy. 10. Parking with restaurants and lodging a short distance away on Hwy. 10.

In Eleva, enter the trail off Hwy. 93 between Hwy. 10 and the river. There is parking on the shoulder and a store nearby.

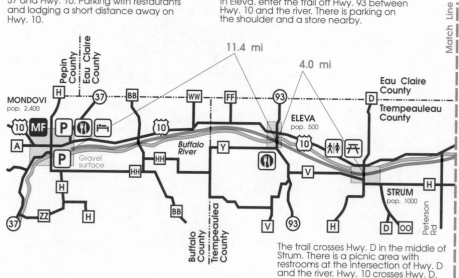

The trail crosses Hwy. D in the middle of Strum. There is a picnic area with restrooms at the intersection of Hwy. D and the river. Hwy. 10 crosses Hwy. D.

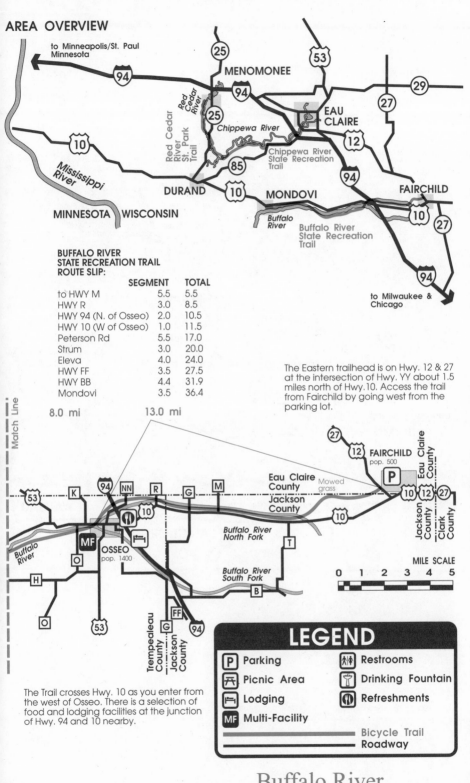

AREA OVERVIEW

to Minneapolis/St. Paul
Minnesota

MENOMONEE

Red Cedar River

Red Cedar River St. Park Trail

Chippewa River

EAU CLAIRE

Chippewa River State Recreation Trail

Mississippi River

DURAND

MONDOVI

FAIRCHILD

MINNESOTA   WISCONSIN

Buffalo River

Buffalo River State Recreation Trail

to Milwaukee & Chicago

BUFFALO RIVER STATE RECREATION TRAIL ROUTE SLIP:

	SEGMENT	TOTAL
to HWY M	5.5	5.5
HWY R	3.0	8.5
HWY 94 (N. of Osseo)	2.0	10.5
HWY 10 (W of Osseo)	1.0	11.5
Peterson Rd	5.5	17.0
Strum	3.0	20.0
Eleva	4.0	24.0
HWY FF	3.5	27.5
HWY BB	4.4	31.9
Mondovi	3.5	36.4

The Eastern trailhead is on Hwy. 12 & 27 at the intersection of Hwy. YY about 1.5 miles north of Hwy.10. Access the trail from Fairchild by going west from the parking lot.

8.0 mi   13.0 mi

Match Line

FAIRCHILD
pop. 500

Eau Claire County
Jackson County

Mowed grass

Buffalo River

OSSEO
pop. 1400

Buffalo River North Fork

Buffalo River South Fork

Eau Claire County
Clark County
Jackson County

Trempealeau County
Jackson County

MILE SCALE

0 1 2 3 4 5

LEGEND

	Parking		Restrooms
	Picnic Area		Drinking Fountain
	Lodging		Refreshments
MF	Multi-Facility		

Bicycle Trail
Roadway

The Trail crosses Hwy. 10 as you enter from the west of Osseo. There is a selection of food and lodging facilities at the junction of Hwy. 94 and 10 nearby.

Buffalo River State Recreation Trail

Northern Wisconsin Overview

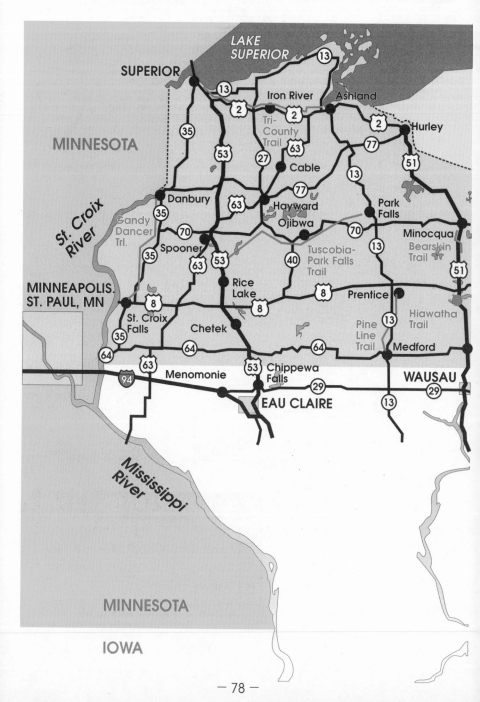

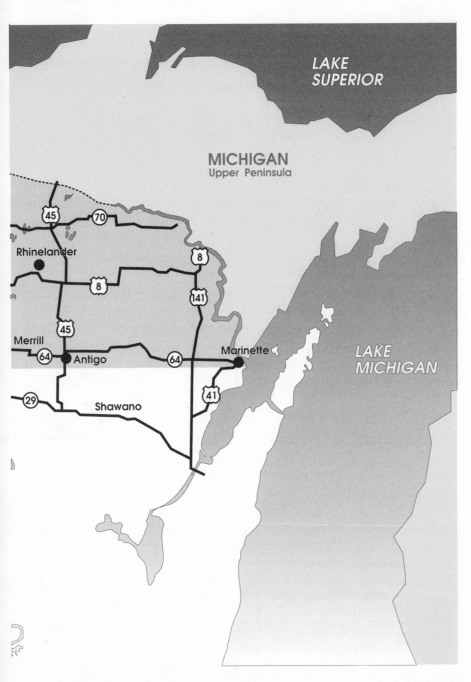

Pine Line Trail

Trail Length	26.1 miles
Surface	Limestone screenings & crushed gravel
Uses	Bicycling, x-c skiing, snowmobiling, hiking
Location & Setting	The Pine Line Trail is in north central Wisconsin, with its southern trailhead in Medford. The trail follows the abandoned Wisconsin Central Railroad right-of-way. The Pine Line has a gentle grade and passes through wooded glacial hills past numerous beaver ponds.
Information	Ice Age Park & Trail Foundation 715/748-2030 Box 339, Medford, WI 54451
Counties	Price, Taylor

AREA OVERVIEW

MEDFORD

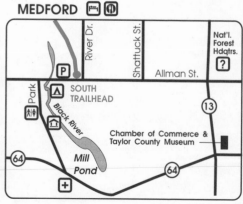

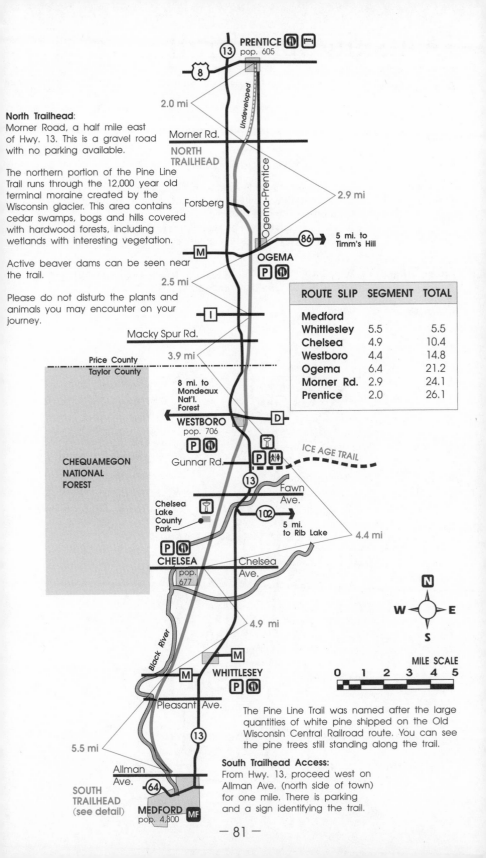

PRENTICE 🏨🛏️
pop. 605
(13)
(8)

2.0 mi

Undeveloped

Morner Rd.
NORTH TRAILHEAD

Ogema-Prentice

Forsberg

2.9 mi

(86) → 5 mi. to Timm's Hill

OGEMA
P 🏨

2.5 mi

[M]

[I]

Macky Spur Rd.

3.9 mi

Price County
Taylor County

8 mi. to Mondeaux Nat'l. Forest

← **WESTBORO**
pop. 706
P 🏨

[D]

Gunnar Rd.

P 🚶
ICE AGE TRAIL

CHEQUAMEGON NATIONAL FOREST

(13)
Fawn Ave.

Chelsea Lake County Park —

(102) → 5 mi. to Rib Lake

4.4 mi

P 🏨
CHELSEA
pop. 677

Chelsea Ave.

Black River

4.9 mi

[M]
[M] **WHITTLESEY**
P 🏨

Pleasant Ave.

(13)

5.5 mi

Allman Ave.
(64)
SOUTH TRAILHEAD
(see detail)

MEDFORD [MF]
pop. 4,800

North Trailhead:
Morner Road, a half mile east of Hwy. 13. This is a gravel road with no parking available.

The northern portion of the Pine Line Trail runs through the 12,000 year old terminal moraine created by the Wisconsin glacier. This area contains cedar swamps, bogs and hills covered with hardwood forests, including wetlands with interesting vegetation.

Active beaver dams can be seen near the trail.

Please do not disturb the plants and animals you may encounter on your journey.

ROUTE SLIP	SEGMENT	TOTAL
Medford		
Whittlesley	5.5	5.5
Chelsea	4.9	10.4
Westboro	4.4	14.8
Ogema	6.4	21.2
Morner Rd.	2.9	24.1
Prentice	2.0	26.1

N
W—E
S

MILE SCALE
0 1 2 3 4 5

The Pine Line Trail was named after the large quantities of white pine shipped on the Old Wisconsin Central Railroad route. You can see the pine trees still standing along the trail.

South Trailhead Access:
From Hwy. 13, proceed west on Allman Ave. (north side of town) for one mile. There is parking and a sign identifying the trail.

– 81 –

Bearskin State Trail

Trail Length	18.3 miles
Surface	Crushed granite
Uses	Bicycling, hiking, snowmobiling
Location & Setting	The Bearskin State Trail is located in north central Wisconsin. The northern trailhead and an information center are located in Minocqua. The trail proceeds south to Hwy. K about 12 miles west of Rhinelander. The Bearskin Trail was built on an abandoned railroad line and is named after Bearskin Creek, a tributary of the Tomahawk River it traverses.
Information	Wisconsin Department of Natural Resources 715/385-2727 4125 CTH M,Boulder Junction, WI 54512
Counties	Oneida

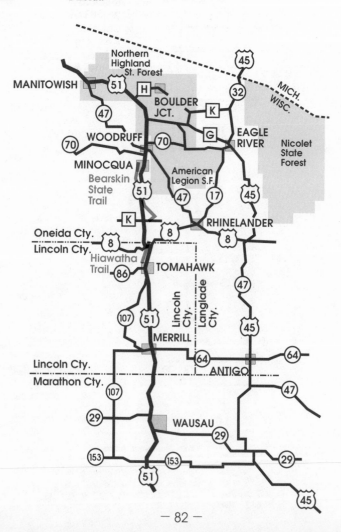

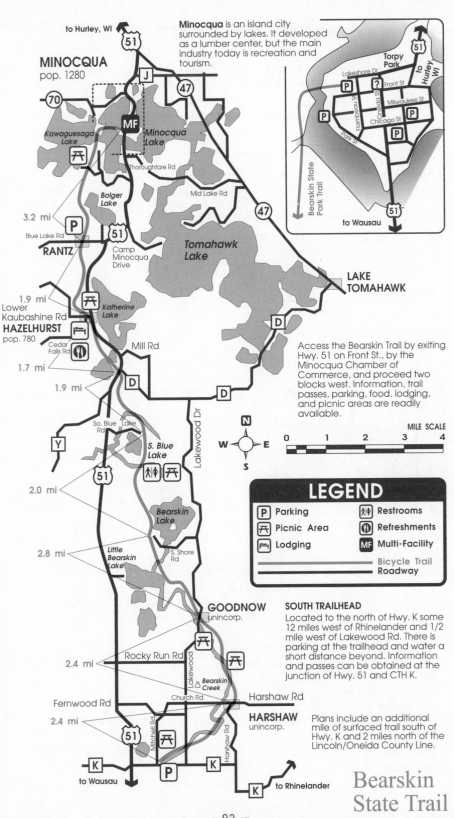

Minocqua is an island city surrounded by lakes. It developed as a lumber center, but the main industry today is recreation and tourism.

to Hurley, WI
51

MINOCQUA
pop. 1280

70

J
47

MF

Kawaguesaga Lake

Minocqua Lake

Thoroughfare Rd

Bolger Lake

Mid Lake Rd

47

Tomahawk Lake

3.2 mi

P

Blue Lake Rd

RANTZ

51

Camp Minocqua Drive

LAKE TOMAHAWK

1.9 mi
Lower Kaubashine Rd

Katherine Lake

HAZELHURST
pop. 780

D

Cedar Falls Rd

1.7 mi

Mill Rd

1.9 mi

D

D

Lakewood Dr

So. Blue Lake Rd

S. Blue Lake

Y

51

2.0 mi

Bearskin Lake

2.8 mi

Little Bearskin Lake

S. Shore Rd

Torpy Park

51
to Hurley WI

Lakeshore Dr

P

? Front St

Milwaukee St

P

Chicago St

P

P

Park St

Bearskin State Park Trail

to Wausau

51

Access the Bearskin Trail by exiting Hwy. 51 on Front St., by the Minocqua Chamber of Commerce, and proceed two blocks west. Information, trail passes, parking, food, lodging, and picnic areas are readily available.

MILE SCALE
0   1   2   3   4

N
W   E
S

LEGEND
P Parking — 👫 Restrooms
🎋 Picnic Area — 🔟 Refreshments
🛏 Lodging — MF Multi-Facility
Bicycle Trail
Roadway

GOODNOW
unincorp.

SOUTH TRAILHEAD
Located to the north of Hwy. K some 12 miles west of Rhinelander and 1/2 mile west of Lakewood Rd. There is parking at the trailhead and water a short distance beyond. Information and passes can be obtained at the junction of Hwy. 51 and CTH K.

Rocky Run Rd

2.4 mi

Lakewood Dr

Bearskin Creek

Fernwood Rd

Church Rd

Harshaw Rd

2.4 mi

51

Mitchell Rd

HARSHAW
unincorp.

Harshaw Rd

K

P

K

K
to Rhinelander

to Wausau

Plans include an additional mile of surfaced trail south of Hwy. K and 2 miles north of the Lincoln/Oneida County Line.

Bearskin State Trail

Tuscobia-Park Falls State Trail

Trail Length	74 miles
Surface	Loose gravel, cinders
Uses	Bicycling, x-c skiing, snowmobiling, hiking, ATV
Location & Setting	The trail consists of abandoned railbed and runs from Park Falls at the eastern trailhead to Tuscobia, a few miles north of Rice Lake, at the western trailhead. The setting is primarily open area, lightly wooded, and small communities.
Information	Tuscobia Trail DNR P.O. Box 187, Winter, WI 54896 715/634-6513
Counties	Price, Sawyer, Washburn, Barron

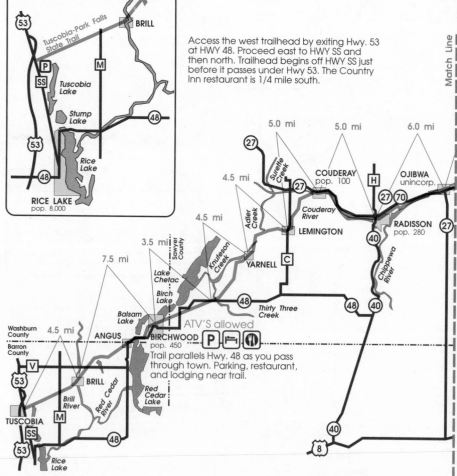

WEST TRAILHEAD

Access the west trailhead by exiting Hwy. 53 at HWY 48. Proceed east to HWY SS and then north. Trailhead begins off HWY SS just before it passes under Hwy 53. The Country Inn restaurant is 1/4 mile south.

ATV'S allowed

Trail parallels Hwy. 48 as you pass through town. Parking, restaurant, and lodging near trail.

TUSCOBIA-PARK FALLS STATE TRAIL ROUTE SLIP:

Park Falls	SEGMENT	TOTAL
Kaiser Rd.	3.5	3.5
Log Creek	9.0	12.5
Draper	6.0	18.5
Loretta	1.0	19.5
Winter (HWY W)	9.0	28.5
Ojibwa	5.0	33.5
Radisson	6.0	39.5
Couderay	5.0	44.5
Lemington (HWY C)	5.0	49.5
Yarnell Rd. (N/S)	4.5	54.0
HWY 48 (E/W)	4.5	58.5
Birchwood	3.5	62.0
Brill (27th Ave.)	7.5	69.5
HWY 53	4.5	74.0

Access trailhead by turning west off Hwy. 13 at Division Street and proceed 5 blocks to 9th Avenue. Trail is 1 block south of Division Street.

PARK FALLS EAST TRAILHEAD

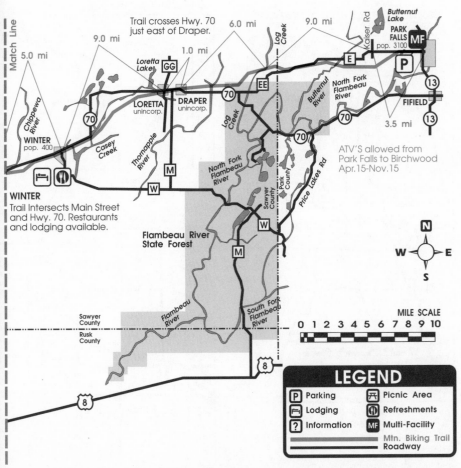

Trail crosses Hwy. 70 just east of Draper.

ATV'S allowed from Park Falls to Birchwood Apr.15-Nov.15

WINTER
Trail Intersects Main Street and Hwy. 70. Restaurants and lodging available.

MILE SCALE
0 1 2 3 4 5 6 7 8 9 10

LEGEND

P	Parking	🏓	Picnic Area
🛏	Lodging	🍴	Refreshments
?	Information	MF	Multi-Facility
			Mtn. Biking Trail
			Roadway

Tuscobia-Park Falls State Trail

Gandy Dancer Trail

Trail Length	48 miles
Surface	Crushed limestone
Uses	Bicycling, hiking, x-c skiing, snowmobiling
Location & Setting	The Gandy Dancer Trail is located in northwest Wisconsin near the Minnesota state line, running north/south between Danbury and St. Croix Falls. The setting is rural, small towns, and agricultural. Built on converted railbed.

Information

Polk County Tourism
Polk County Courthouse
Balsam Lake, WI 54810

800/222-7655 or
715/485-3161

Burnett County Tourism
Route 1, Box 300-112R, Siren, WI 54872

800/788-3164

Counties   Polk, Burnett

**NORTHWEST WISCONSIN OVERVIEW
GANDY DANCER TRAIL**

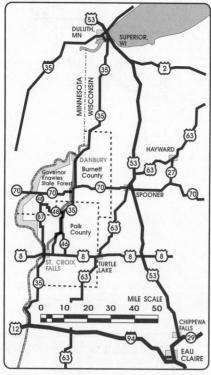

The Gandy Dancer Trail stretches from St. Croix Falls to Danbury, through Polk and Burnett counties. It was developed on abandoned Soo Line railbed. The distances between the towns along the trail are never more than 10 miles apart. There are park and rest areas along the trail.

DANBURY

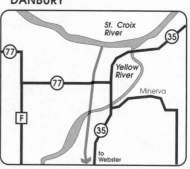

The north trailhead in Danbury is at Hwy. 77, 1 block west of Hwy. 35.

ST. CROIX FALLS

From St. Croix Falls, the trail can be accessed from Maple Drive or Pine Avenue.

The Gandy Dancer Trail was named for the railroad workers who used tools from the Gandy Tool Company and came to be known as Gandy Dancers.

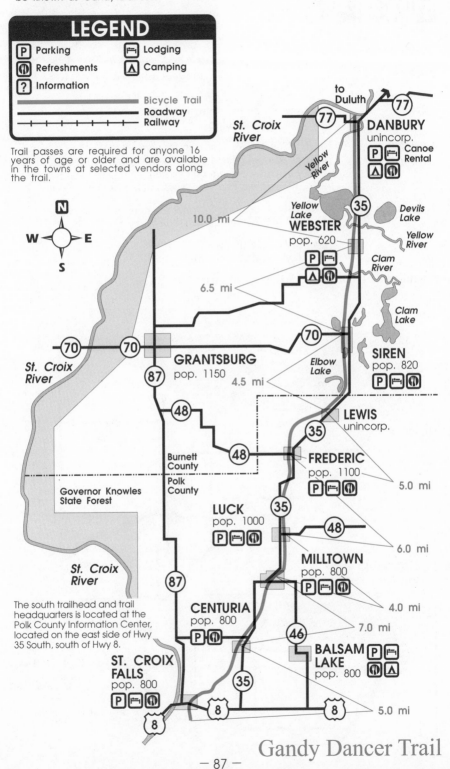

LEGEND

P	Parking	🛏	Lodging
🍴	Refreshments	▲	Camping
?	Information		

Bicycle Trail
Roadway
Railway

Trail passes are required for anyone 16 years of age or older and are available in the towns at selected vendors along the trail.

N
W E
S

to Duluth

DANBURY
unincorp.
P 🛏 Canoe Rental
▲ 🍴

St. Croix River

Yellow River

Yellow Lake

Devils Lake

WEBSTER
pop. 620
P 🛏
▲ 🍴

Yellow River

Clam River

10.0 mi

6.5 mi

Clam Lake

70

SIREN
pop. 820
P 🛏 🍴

GRANTSBURG
pop. 1150

St. Croix River

Elbow Lake

4.5 mi

LEWIS
unincorp.

FREDERIC
pop. 1100
P 🛏 🍴

5.0 mi

Burnett County
Polk County

LUCK
pop. 1000
P 🛏 🍴

6.0 mi

Governor Knowles State Forest

MILLTOWN
pop. 800
P 🛏 🍴

4.0 mi

St. Croix River

CENTURIA
pop. 800
P 🍴

7.0 mi

The south trailhead and trail headquarters is located at the Polk County Information Center, located on the east side of Hwy 35 South, south of Hwy 8.

BALSAM LAKE P 🛏
pop. 800 🍴 ▲

ST. CROIX FALLS
pop. 800
P 🛏 🍴

5.0 mi

Gandy Dancer Trail

Tri-County Corridor

Trail Length	60 miles
Surface	Screenings - There is 1.3 miles of asphalt from Superior trailhead
Uses	Bicycling, x-c skiing, snowmobiling, hiking, horseback riding
Location & Setting	The Tri-County Corridor is in far northwest Wisconsin between Superior and Ashland. The trail is on abandoned railbed. The Tri-County Corridor provides a panoramic view of local farm and forest, with only a few small communities along the route.
Information	Tri-County Recreation Corridor Commission *no phone* P.O. Box 503, Ashland, WI 54806 Superior Parks & Recreation 715/394-0270 1407 Hammond Avenue, Superior, WI 54880
Counties	Bayfield, Douglas, Ashland

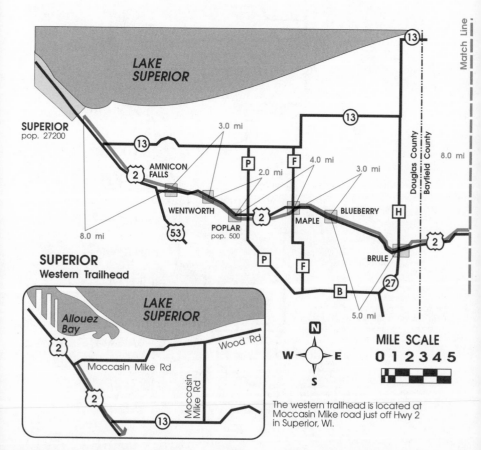

The western trailhead is located at Moccasin Mike road just off Hwy 2 in Superior, WI.

The Tri-County Recreational Corridor serves as a major connector route to the hundreds of miles of recreational trails in Northwest Wisconsin. It links extensive snowmobile trails throughout Douglas, Ashland, and Bayfield counties, as well as those going as far south as the Twin Cities.

AREA OVERVIEW

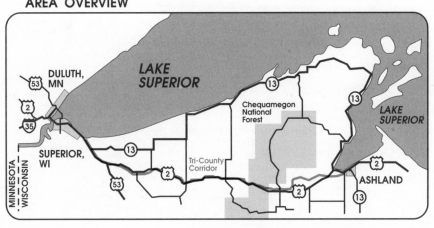

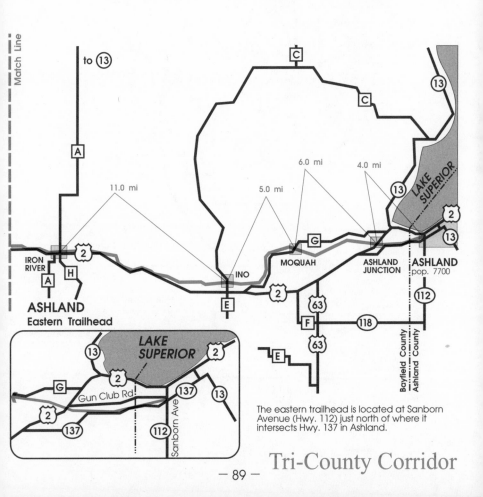

The eastern trailhead is located at Sanborn Avenue (Hwy. 112) just north of where it intersects Hwy. 137 in Ashland.

Tri-County Corridor

Hiawatha Trail

Trail Length	6.6 miles
Surface	Screenings (rotten granite)
Uses	Bicycling, x-c skiing, snowmobiling, hiking
Location & Setting	The Hiawatha Trail is located in Lincoln County in north central Wisconsin. Sara Park in Tomahawk is the southern trailhead. It follows the abandoned Milwaukee Road railbed to the county line near Lake Nokomis. The setting is lakeland and open areas.
Information	Tomahawk Chamber of commerce 715/453-5334 208 North 4th Street, P.O. Box 412 Tomahawk, WI 54487
County	Lincoln

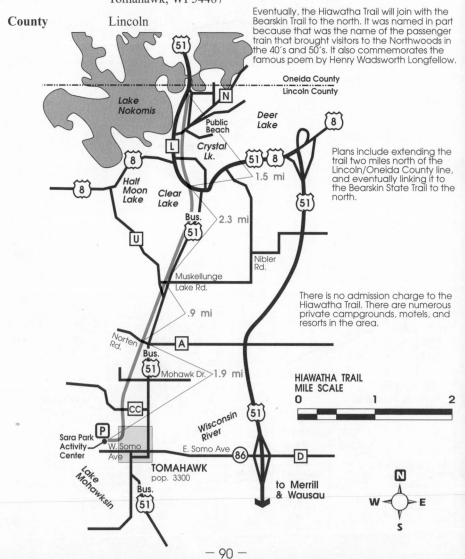

Eventually, the Hiawatha Trail will join with the Bearskin Trail to the north. It was named in part because that was the name of the passenger train that brought visitors to the Northwoods in the 40's and 50's. It also commemorates the famous poem by Henry Wadsworth Longfellow.

Plans include extending the trail two miles north of the Lincoln/Oneida County line, and eventually linking it to the Bearskin State Trail to the north.

There is no admission charge to the Hiawatha Trail. There are numerous private campgrounds, motels, and resorts in the area.

HIAWATHA TRAIL
MILE SCALE
0   1   2

Trail Log

Trail Name	Page Ref.	General Description: (scenery, conditions, etc.)	Mileage	Date

The Bicycle Federation of Wisconsin
Bicycle Trails Don't Just Happen
by Michael D. Barrett

All of the trails highlighted in this book share in a common idea: The idea that a trail dedicated to human-powered mobility could bring a community together. To be sure, recreation, exercise, clean transportation, and environment all figure into the trail equation, but ultimately, *community is what these trails are all about.*

Many of the trails included here are abandoned rail corridors which have been converted into biking and hiking trails - commonly referred to as rail trails. All of the trails, whether rail trails, corridors in a park, or connectors between cul-de-sacs in subdivisions have succeeded beyond the dreams of even the most ardent supporters.

Communities along the trails are rightly proud of their trails. The trail is often a means to showcase the specialness of their place. But rail trails and other linear park trails did not just happen; they are the product of the imagination and dedication of civic-minded folks.

The idea of a rail-to-trail conversion has been around for a while, beginning with central Wisconsin's Elroy-Sparta Trail in the mid-1960's. However, the current network of hundreds of trail miles did not blossom until the 1990's. Why did it take so long to get going? Money.

Communities Take Charge
Though the success of the Elroy-Sparta trail in boosting local economies was well-known, the ability of other small towns to harness the funds for trails was limited...until the passage of the landmark 1991 Intermodal Surface Transportation Efficiency Act (ISTEA).

Before your eyes glaze over from the bureaucratese, here is a summation: Prior to the passage of ISTEA all federal transportation funds given over to local governments had to be spent on highways. With ISTEA, local governments could use a small percentage of their transportation funds on other modes, such as walking and biking. Trails flourished. Flexible transportation dollars meant that pent-up citizen demand for community-friendly biking and walking facilities could be met. The rapid expansion of "human power only" trails is the direct result of greater local control over transportation funds.

Bike Trails Under Fire
Local control over transportation money has come up against serious opposition in recent election cycles. Yet the discussion has nothing to do with budget cutting; it is a question of where the dollars will go, not how much will be spent. The transportation pie will stay the same size, whether ISTEA survives or not. Legislators from the major parties have stated that if there is

enough citizen input for continued local control (for bike and pedestrian projects) under ISTEA, they will support it. So if you would like to see more of these trails, **let your legislator know that ISTEA should continue, bicycle funding included.**

Remember: *Once these linear corridors - heirlooms of our railroading past and connections to our communities' future - are lost, they are gone forever.*

The Bicycle Federation of Wisconsin and Livable Communities
The way to have your voice heard is to join an organization which firmly supports community control of ISTEA funds. In Wisconsin, the major proponent of ISTEA is the **Bicycle Federation of Wisconsin** (the **League of American Bicyclists** and **Rails-to-Trails Conservancy** have been quite effective on the national level).

The Bicycle Federation of Wisconsin, a statewide non-profit, membership-based organization, firmly believes that *the more people on bikes, the more livable the community.* The notion of bikeability and livability is what propels the BFW into the thick of the struggle to maintain community control over ISTEA funds. Over the past five years communities have made the clear choice to rebuild their human-scaled infrastructure through ISTEA; the BFW wants this to continue.

Safe Roads for All
The Bicycle Federation of Wisconsin is also heavily involved in bicycle safety issues, such as education of motorists about cyclists' rights to the road, and effective cycling techniques for cyclists of all ages. The Bicycle Federation of Wisconsin won a major legislative victory in 1996 with the passage of the Bicycle Safety Bill (AB 96), which provided for uniform and updated statutes regarding bicyclists statewide. The bicycle is now clearly and definitively a legal vehicle with all of the rights and responsibilities of any other road user.

Currently the Bicycle Federation of Wisconsin is a member of the State Bicycle Advisory Committee. The Bicycle Federation of Wisconsin is pressing for the State Bike Plan to forthrightly state that bicyclists will be seriously considered in all state-sponsored road projects.

Members Are Our Strength
The Bicycle Federation is membership driven. Please join us in the push for community friendly transportation. *Bicycle Federation of Wisconsin is a membership organization which promotes bikeable communities. Annual memberships are $25 (a personal benefit is a 10 % discount at 35 bike shops and bike-friendly businesses statewide). Inquiries can be addressed* to:

Bicycle Federation of Wisconsin
104 King St., Suite 204
PO. Box 1224, Madison, WI 53701   (608) 251-4456
E-mail: bfw@mailbag. com.

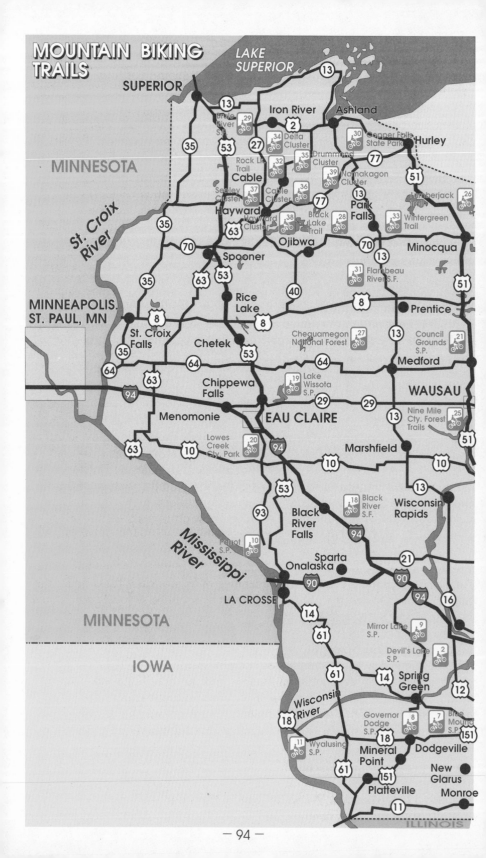

Mountain Biking Alternatives

 BONG STATE RECREATION AREA
Length	12.0 miles
Effort Level	Easy
Setting	Level to rolling terrain. Prairie, woodlands, wetlands.
Location	From Kenosha, 16 miles west on Hwy. 142 to entrance. From Burlington, 8 miles southeast on Hwy. 142.
Park Office	414/652-0377 or 414/878-5600

 DEVIL'S LAKE STATE PARK
Length	6.5 miles
Effort Level	Easy to Difficult
Setting	A generally medium effort trail that is long, winding and grassy, with variable grades through fields, bushy areas and woods. Scenic views from the top of the East Bluff on the south end.
Location	Three miles south of Baraboo on Hwy. 123.
Park Office	608/356-8301

 HARRINGTON BEACH STATE PARK
Trail Length	2.0 miles
Effort Level	Easy
Setting	Grass, sand, lake shore
Location	Ten miles north of Port Washington on Hwy. 43 and then east on Hwy.D for 1 mile.
Park Office	414/285-3015

 KOHLER-ANDRAE STATE PARK
Trail Length	2.5 miles
Effort Level	Easy
Setting	Grassy
Location	Four miles north of Sheboygan on Hwy. 43, and then 2 miles east on Park Drive.
Park Office	414/452-3457

 KETTLE MORAINE - NORTHERN UNIT
Park Office	414/626-2116

GREENBUSH RECREATION AREA
Trail Length	10.9 miles
Effort Level	Easy to difficult
Setting	Hills, woods, grassy areas
Location	Hwy. 23 west to Kettle Moraine Drive at the small town of Greenbush, and then south for 2 miles.

NEW FANE TRAILS
Trail Length	7.7 miles
Effort Level	Easy to difficult
Setting	Hilly, woods, grassy areas
Location	From Milwaukee, take Hwy. 45 north approximately 35 miles to County Route H. East on H for 2 miles to Kettle Moraine Drive, and then north for 3 miles.

 KETTLE MORAINE - SOUTHERN UNIT
Park Office	414/594-2135
Touring Ctr	414/495-8600

JOHN MUIR TRAILS
Trail Length	28.2 miles
Effort Level	Easy to difficult
Setting	Hilly, rocky, open fields, woods
Location	From Milwaukee, take Hwy. 43 southwest to State Route 20 about 9 miles to where it joins Hwy. 12. West on 12 less than 2 miles to County Route H, and then north to the entrance. From Chicago, northwest on Hwy. 12.

EMMA F. CARLIN TRAILS

Trail Length	9.4 miles
Effort Level	Easy to difficult
Setting	Hilly, woods
Location	From Milwaukee, take Hwy. 43 southwest to the town of Mukwonago. Pick up County Route NN north of town and proceed west 5 miles to Eagle. Continue west on State Route 59 for 4 miles to Carlin Trail Road, and then south to the entrance.

LAPHAM PEAK UNIT

Trail Length	4.4 miles
Effort Level	Easy to moderate
Setting	Hills, woods, fields
Location	Seven miles west of Waukesha on Hwy. 94, and then south 1 mile on County Hwy. C.
Forest Office	414/896-8007

SOUTHWEST
BLUE MOUND STATE PARK

Trail Length	4.0 miles
Effort Level	Easy to difficult
Setting	Grass, woods, steep hills
Location	One mile northwest of the town of Blue Mounds off Hwy. 18/15.
Park Office	608/437-5711

GOVERNOR DODGE STATE PARK

Trail Length	10 miles
Effort Level	Moderate
Setting	Meadows, wooded ridges and valleys
Location	Three miles north of Dodgeville on Hwy. 23.
Park Office	608/935-2315

MIRROR LAKE STATE PARK

Trail Length	9.2 miles
Effort Level	Easy to moderate
Setting	Woods, gravel, sand
Location	One and a half miles southwest of Lake Delton on Ishnala Road. Exit Hwy. 94 at Hwy. 12 and proceed south for 1 mile to Fern Dell Road. There is an entrance at the Hastings Road intersection.
Park Office	608/254-2333

PERROT STATE PARK

Trail Length	6 miles
Effort Level	Moderate to difficult
Setting	Hardpacked ski trails. Marshland, prairie, wooded slopes
Location	From LaCrosse, take Hwy. 35 north and then west to Hwy. 93 at Centerville. Proceed south on 93 for 4.5 miles to Trempealeau Follow park signs. From Winona, cross Hwy. 43 bridge and take Hwy. 35 east 10 miles to Centerville.
Park Office	608/534-6409

WYALUSING STATE PARK

Trail Length	11.6 miles
Effort Level	Easy to difficult
Setting	Woods, grassy areas, gently rolling to steep slopes.
Location	Seven miles south of Prairie Du Chien on Hwy. 18, then west on Hwy. C.
Park Office	608/996-2261

NORTHEAST
HIGH CLIFF STATE PARK

Trail Length	8.2 miles
Effort Level	Easy
Setting	Woods, cliffs, lakefront
Location	Three miles south of Hwy. 55 from the town of Sherwood. At High Cliff Road turn left to enter park. Sherwood is about 12 miles southeast of Appleton.
Park Office	414/989-1349

OCONTO COUNTY TRAIL
Trail Length   30 miles
Effort Level   Easy
Setting   Forests, farmland, small communities. Trail is on abandoned railbed.
Location   Trail runs from Gillett to Lakewood. Gillett is located 14 miles west of Hwy.
                    141 on Hwy. 22, and is approximately 42 miles northwest of Green Bay.
Park Office   414/834-6820

NEWPORT STATE PARK
Trail Length   12 miles
Effort Level   Easy
Setting   Forests, wetlands, meadows
Location   Door County, 2 miles east of Ellison Bay on Hwy 22, and then 2 miles southeast
                    on Hwy. Z.
Information   414/854-2500

PENINSULA STATE PARK
Trail Length   12.8 miles
Effort Level   Easy to moderate
Setting   Forest, meadows marsh, cliffs
Location   Door County, 3 miles north of Fish Creek off Hwy. 42.
Park Office   414/868-3258

POTAWATOMI STATE PARK
Trail Length   4 miles
Effort Level   Moderate
Setting   Flat to gently rolling upland terrain, bordered by steep slopes and cliffs.
Location   Door County, 5 miles northwest of Sturgeon Bay. Take Hwy. 42/57 west to Park
                    Road, and then north to park entrance.
Park Office   414/746-2890

POINT BEACH STATE FOREST
Trail Length   4 miles
Effort Level   Moderate
Setting   Forest bordered by sand beaches.
Location   Four miles north of Two Rivers, off County Hwy. O.
Park Office   414/794-7480

WEST CENTRAL
BLACK RIVER STATE FOREST

Forest Office   715/284-1400

CASTLE MOUND PARK
Trail Length   4.5 miles
Effort Level   Easy
Setting   Generally level with grassy surface, but some hills.
Location   1.5 miles southeast of Black River Falls on Hwy. 12.

PIGEON CREEK
Trail Length   4 miles
Effort Level   Easy
Setting   Fairly level terrain with mostly grassy surface
Location   Twelve miles southeast of Black River Falls on Hwy. 12 to Hwy. O, then 4 miles
                    northeast to North Settlement Road.

SMREKAR TRAIL
Trail Length   7.5 miles
Effort Level   Moderate to difficult
Setting   Wooded, ridges
Location   Twelve miles southeast of Black River Falls on Hwy. 12 to Hwy. O, then 4 miles
                    northeast to North Settlement Road. Continue northeast.

WILDCAT TRAIL
Trail Length	7.5 miles
Effort Level	Moderate to difficult
Setting	Heavy woods, buttes and sandstone hills
Location	Twelve miles southeast of Black River Falls on Hwy. 12 to Hwy O, then 4 miles northeast to North Settlement Road. Continue northeast.

LAKE WISSOTA STATE PARK
Trail Length	11 miles
Effort Level	Easy
Setting	Most prairie grass and plantation pines
Location	Eight miles northeast of Chippewa Falls. North on Hwy. 53 to County Road 3, then east. Turn right on County Road S and continue 1.7 miles to the park entrance.
Park Office	715/382-4574

LOWES CREEK COUNTY PARK
Trail Length	4.9 miles
Effort Level	Easy to difficult
Setting	The West Loop is rolling and prairie. The East Loop is wooded. The trail loop between the East and West Loop is flat and mostly open.
Location	One and a third miles west of Hwy. 93 on Hwy. 94 to Lowes Creek Road, then south 1.5 miles to park entrance.
Park Office	715/839-4738

NORTH CENTRAL
COUNCIL GROUNDS STATE PARK
Trail Length	2.5 miles
Effort Level	Easy
Setting	Heavily wooded
Location	One mile west of Merrill on Hwy. 107
Park Office	715/536-8773

LUMBERJACK TRAIL
Trail Length	12 miles
Effort Level	Easy to moderate
Setting	Gently rolling, heavily wooded
Location	From Boulder Junction, south 1 mile on old Hwy. K to Concora Road; or approximately 6 miles southeast of Boulder Junction on County Hwy. K to the east side of White Sand Lake.
Park Office	715/356-5211

MADELINE LAKE TRAIL
Trail Length	9.5 miles
Effort Level	Easy to moderate
Setting	Level to rolling terrain
Location	Two miles southeast of Woodruff. Take Hwy. 51 to Hwy. J. East on J to Rudolph Road and then north to trail.
Information	715/356-5211

McNAUGHTON LAKE TRAILS
Trail Length	7.0 miles
Effort Level	Easy
Setting	Gentle terrain with a few steep hills. Dirt and mowed grass.
Location	Thirteen miles south of Woodruff. Take Hwy. 47 east, through Lake Tomahawk. Turn right on Kildare Road.
Information	715/356-5211

NINE MILE COUNTY FOREST TRAILS
Trail Length	18.5 miles
Effort Level	Easy to difficult
Setting	Wooded uplands, marshes, water impoundments
Location	From Wausau at Hwy. 51, take Hwy. N west approximately 3.5 miles to Red Bud Road, and then south 1.5 miles.
Forest Office	715/847-5267

SHANNON LAKE TRAIL
Trail Length	7.6 miles
Effort Level	Easy to moderate
Setting	Gently rolling and wooded
Location	Two and a half miles northeast of St. Germain. Take Hwy. 155 to Found Lake Road. Another access is approximately 10 miles from Eagle River on Hwy. G.
Information	715/356-5211

CHEQUAMEGON NATIONAL FOREST
Trail Length	Twenty five miles of trails plus over a 100 miles of forest roads
Effort Level	Moderate
Setting	Forest - natural and groomed trails, roads
Location	Taylor and Price County. Located in north central Wisconsin, northwest of Wausau and northeast of Eau Claire.
Information	Chequamegon National Forest, 1170 4th Ave. S, Park Falls, WI 54522

NORTHWEST

BLACK LAKE TRAIL
Trail Length	4.0 miles
Effort Level	Easy
Setting	The trail circles Black Lake. The area was heavily lumbered during the early 1900's. Part of the trail follows an old logging road.
Location	From Hayward, 26 miles east on Hwy. B to the Hwy. W intersection. Turn left (north) on Fishtrap Road for 4.8 miles to Forest Road 172. Continue north 3.3 miles to Forest Road 173, then left for .5 miles to Forest Road 1666 (campground road). Turn right (east) on the blacktop road for .5 miles to a parking lot and trailhead.
Forest Office	715/634-4821

BRULE RIVER STATE FOREST
Trail Length	6.0 miles
Effort Level	Easy to moderate
Setting	Rolling hills, deep forests.
Location	Two miles northwest of Brule on Hwy. 2, then west to trailhead.
Forest Office	715/372-4866

COPPER FALLS STATE PARK
Trail Length	8.3 miles
Setting	Easy to difficult
Setting	Rolling terrain, hilly
Location	Two miles north to Mellon on Hwy. 169, then 2 miles on Hwy. J. The trailhead is west of the main park entrance road about .3 miles from the park office. Take the right trail split.
Park Office	715/463-2898

FLAMBEAU RIVER STATE FOREST
Trail Length	Over 100 miles
Effort Level	Easy to difficult
Setting	Forests
Location	Approximately 10 miles southwest of Park Falls between Hwy. 70 to the north and Hwy. 8 to the south.
Forest Office	715/332-5271

ROCK LAKE TRAIL
Trail Length	25 miles (loops)
Effort Level	Easy to difficult
Setting	Rolling terrain, hills, forested, ridges
Location	Seven and a half miles east of Cable and 12 miles west of Clam Lake on Hwy. M.
Forest Office	715/634-4821

WINTERGREEN TRAIL
Trail Length	15.4 miles
Effort Level	Moderate to difficult
Setting	Forests, Upland ridges to lowland marshes
Location	Five miles east of Fifield and north of Hwy. 70. Fifield is 4 miles south of Park Falls at Hwy. 70 and 13.
Forest Office	715/762-2461

CAMBA TRAILS - NORTHWEST
Information	Chequamegon Area Mountain Bike Association (CAMBA)	800/533-7454

DELTA CLUSTER
Trail Length	65 miles - loops
Effort Level	Easy to difficult single track sections
Location	Between Iron River and Drummond.

DRUMMOND CLUSTER
Trail Length	82 miles - loops
Effort Level	Easy to moderate - road sections & ski trails
Location	Drummond area

CABLE CLUSTER
Trail Length	60 miles - loops
Effort Level	Easy to difficult
Location	South from Cable on Randysek Road less than a mile, then east on McNaught Road to trailhead.

SEELEY CLUSTER
Trail Length	68 miles - loops
Effort Level	Moderate to difficult
Location	Seeley

HAYWARD CLUSTER
Trail Length	34 miles - loops
Effort Level	Easy to moderate
Location	Hayward

NAMAKAGON CLUSTER
Trail Length	42 miles - loops
Effort Level	Easy to difficult
Location	Trailheads are east of Namakagon, off Hwy. M.

ORGANIZATIONS TO CONTACT:
CHEQUAMEGON AREA MOUNTAIN BIKE ASSOCIATION (CAMBA)
This coalition of mountain bikers and Chequamegon area merchants has developed over 300 miles of mapped and marked trails in and around the Chequamegon National Forest in Bayfield and Sawyer Counties.
Address: CAMBA, P.O. Box 141, Cable, WI 54821

WISCONSIN DEPT. OF NATURAL RESOURCES (DNR) Bureau of Parks and Recreation
Address: P.O. Box 7921, Madison, WI 53707-7921

WISCONSIN ENVIRONMENTAL INITIATIVE
A non-profit educational organization bringing diverse groups together in a collaborative, non-contentious forum to facilitate solutions to contemporary regional environmental issues. New in 1996, their first conference was called "Quality Urban Development: Setting an Agenda for Wisconsin's Cities".
Address: 5315 Wall Street, Ste. 235, Madison, WI 53704-7939   Phone 608/249-5834

WISCONSIN OFF-ROAD BICYCLING ASSOCIATION (WORBA)
Promotes trail access, environmentally responsible trail use, and cooperation among all trail user groups to preserve off-road cycling opportunities and green space. This is accomplished through education, advocacy, and volunteer action. Call their **hot line** at 608/251-4911, which is updated with new events.
Address: WORBA, P.O. BOX 1681, Madison, WI 53701

TRAIL INDEX

TRAIL INDEX *(continued)*

Sections: N = North; C = Central; S = South

CITY TO TRAIL INDEX

To order additional copies of this book

Pay by Check or Credit Card

Mail Check to:

American Bike Trails

1157 South Milwaukee Avenue

Libertyville, IL 60048

Book *(per copy)*	$12.95
Handling *(per copy)*	$2.00
Sales Tax - IL residents *(per copy)*	$.85
TOTAL	**$15.80**

To order by Credit Card call (800) 246-4627

American Bike Trails
publishes and distributes maps, books, and guides
for the recreational bicyclist. Our trail maps
cover over 250 trails throughout the states of
Illinois, Iowa, Michigan, Minnesota, and Wisconsin

For a free copy of our catalog write to the above address